DATE DUE

GAYLORD   PRINTED IN U.S.A.

The Gift Outright

AMERICA TO HER POETS

THE GIFT OUTRIGHT

America to Her Poets

Edited by HELEN PLOTZ

GREENWILLOW BOOKS
A Division of William Morrow & Company, Inc.
New York

Pages 199-204 constitute an extension of the copyright page.

For their help in the typing and the
preparation of the manuscript I am
indebted to Rebecca Tope and to
Muriel Golden

10   9   8   7   6   5   4   3   2   1

Library of Congress Cataloging in Publication Data
Main entry under title: The Gift outright.
Summary: An anthology portraying America as seen by
her poets from colonial days to the present time.
1.   American poetry.   2.   United States—Poetry.
[1.   American poetry—Collections.   2.   United States—
Poetry]
I.   Plotz, Helen.
PS595.U5G5   811'.008   77-8555
ISBN 0-688-80109-9
ISBN 0-688-84109-0 lib. bdg.

In memory of Milton
And for our grandchildren

 ❀   *Anne Elizabeth*
 ❀   *Victoria Rose*
 ❀   *John Milton Gabriel*
 ❀   *James David*
 ❀   *David Avrion*

CONTENTS

INTRODUCTION

"The last best hope of earth"—so has America seemed again and again to the world and to herself. It is more than a hundred years since Lincoln said that we would "nobly save or meanly lose" that hope. From the beginning, countless politicians, rebels, patriots and "unpatriots" have exhorted us, praised us, excoriated us, all in the name of the American vision, naming the names of countless heroes and villains to symbolize a fulfillment or a betrayal of that vision.

And the poets—what of them? America's poets from the seventeenth century until the present day have been caught up in the American dream. From the earliest days of colonization, America has spoken to her poets and through her poets. In doggerel, ballads and high-flown classical verse, in rhymed verse, blank verse and free verse, our poets have concerned themselves with the definition of America, of the American promise. Many poets have railed against America, but their anger has been directed against the betrayers of the American ideal. I have not found a single poem directed against that ideal.

Not by chance was America called "The New World." The lost continent of Atlantis, described by Plato, lay to the west of the Pillars of Hercules, as Canaan, the Promised Land of the Bible, lay to the west of the River Jordan. In all the history of western civilization, the West has been and remains the symbol of an earthly paradise. English poetry is full of allusions to the West, from Shakespeare's "Westward Ho," to Wordsworth's "Stepping Westward," to Clough's "Westward look, the land is bright"—and, naturally, even more than English poetry, American poetry is suffused with the lure of the West. In this gathering of poems by American poets there are two themes that persist: America as Geography and America as Idea. These themes are intertwined and inseparable one from the other, so that the Statue of Liberty and the Mississippi River, Monticello and the Golden Gate, shape and are shaped by the American experience and have a symbolic as well as an actual existence.

This land, this New World, was named not for its discoverer, but for a merchant-adventurer who claimed its discovery. Amerigo Vespucci's claim was strengthened by a professor of cosmography and so the new land came to be called the land of Americus, although many poets have called her "Columbia."

To begin with Columbus, as indeed we must, we can find in his voyages the seed of all that was to come. True, he sought the East and named the people he found here "Indians." He found the West.

The first group of poems are about Columbus, the Admiral of the Ocean Sea, the true discoverer of America; whether the Vikings landed in the North, whether Vespucci landed somewhere on our coast, is irrelevant. Within a hundred years, the European settlements began—St. Augustine, Santa Fe, New Amsterdam, Jamestown and Plymouth. The New World was within reach of the Old. The making of this world was accomplished by violence and treachery as well as by suffering and courage and idealism. This has been told over and over in the documents of the time, in our history books and in our geographies. And it has been told and is being told by our poets.

The people whom Columbus named "Indians" occupied

the islands and the continent of North America. We call them Indians, or Amerindians. They prefer, nowadays, to be known as "Native Americans," a more accurate designation, to be sure, and one with which many agree. Nevertheless, they are still called Indians and poems about them form the second section of this book. I have singled out the Indians because their relationship to America is unique. Wherever they came from, whenever they came, is not our present concern. What matters is that they were here before the Europeans. Sometimes the Europeans were incredibly insensitive to the needs of the Indians; certainly there is much evidence of injustice on the part of the whites. Indians have often been sentimentalized as "Noble Savages," a not too subtle denigration, and sometimes have been stigmatized as bloodthirsty barbarians, destined to lose in the game of "Cowboys and Indians" and then to bite the dust forever. Some of the poems I have chosen for this section reflect these derogatory attitudes, but there are many poems, some from the colonists' earliest days here, which are thoughtful and compassionate. This section also includes poems by the Indians themselves. It is worth remembering that our most distinctively American symbols, the buffalo and the eagle, are Indian emblems too.

The third section is devoted to the settlers, who they were and how they came, some in the slave ships, some on the *Mayflower*, some in steerage, some as prisoners, some as bondsmen and women, some as conquerors. We call them by various names. Depending on our own attitudes, we call them "Pilgrim Fathers," "O Pioneers," "Greenhorns," "Refugees," "Wretched Refuse." What we euphemistically call "ethnic slurs"—no need to list them, they are all too familiar to most of us—are also used to describe the people who have followed the westward, and sometimes the eastward, path to freedom.

This path was not followed by the blacks who were brought here not for freedom, but for slavery. That they achieved freedom and achieved it before slavery was abolished in Africa and Asia, is perhaps the most amazing of all American miracles. This is not to say that the struggle is over or all the battles won—far from it. Nevertheless, Martin Luther King's dream will be realized in America.

The trek to the West and the legends that sprang up around it are the subject of the next section—the story of the regions. The earliest settlements were not in Massachusetts and Virginia, but in Florida (1565) and New Mexico (1598). The surge was westward. Daniel Boone, Davy Crockett, Lewis and Clark, Buffalo Bill are names we have heard all our lives. The covered wagon and the railroads are part of our expanding country.

If it seems that it all started in New England and Virginia, that is a natural enough assumption, which arises from two circumstances. We are an English-speaking country with the infinite riches of the English language ours to use, to add to and sometimes to change. The other link is our legal system, which derives from the English system. So, in a sense, England is the mother country of us all.

Yet this country is so large, so varied in its geography, that its many regions have their own traditions, their own needs, their own idiom. There are the East and the West and, flowing between them, the mightiest of our rivers, the Mississippi. There are the North and the South. Once, in our greatest national tragedy, these regions faced each other in a deadly war. Such a profound division did not occur again until the Vietnam War tore us asunder and once more set brother against brother and friend against friend.

The fifth section has to do with the men and women and the events which shaped our country, with our Presidents, with the wars we have fought, with our political heritage and with some of the terrible injustices we have tolerated. There have been times when our betrayers have masqueraded as our saviors. Some of the wrongs perpetrated in the name of Americanism are irremediable. Yet we have survived these wrongs. Thomas Paine, in the days of the Revolution, said, "These are the times that try men's souls." Our poets speak of America in the language of their own times: Philip Freneau and Lawrence Ferlinghetti have the same concerns, the same passionate involvement.

America as Idea, as Dream, has pervaded all the poems in this book. The last section deals with the ideas in abstract rather than concrete terms. Here the poet asks himself "What is an American?"—a question never to be answered once and for all, for each generation must redefine its ideals. It is the fashion, in some circles, to analyze the American Revolution as a movement of propertied men, eager to preserve their material comforts and to hold off the rabble. If that were all, we should not have come through these two hundred years.

The meaning of this book lies in a poem by Robert Frost. Let the book begin with it.

THE GIFT OUTRIGHT

The land was ours before we were the land's.
She was our land more than a hundred years
Before we were her people. She was ours
In Massachusetts, in Virginia,
But we were England's, still colonials,
Possessing what we still were unpossessed by,
Possessed by what we now no more possessed.
Something we were withholding made us weak
Until we found it was ourselves
We were withholding from our land of living,
And forthwith found salvation in surrender.
Such as we were we gave ourselves outright
(The deed of gift was many deeds of war)
To the land vaguely realizing westward,
But still unstoried, artless, unenhanced,
Such as she was, such as she would become.

ROBERT FROST

You, Genoese Mariner

✱ COLUMBUS

YOU, GENOESE MARINER

You, Genoese mariner,
Your face most perfectly
A mask about a vision,
Your eyes most clear when turned
On the bewildering west,
You, so your story goes,
Who believed that that direction
Toward which all breath and knowledge
Although their eyes cling elsewhere
Make ignorant declension,
Must by its own token,
Continuing, contain
A grammar of return,
A world's unknown dimension,
You, nevertheless, in search
Of gilt and spice, who fancied
Earth too circumscribed
To imagine and cradle,
Where no map had suspected,
The distances and marvels,
The unfingered world—
I whose face has become,
Oh mistaken sailor,
Suddenly a frame
For astonishment, stand
In the long light of wonder
Staring upon the shadows
That circle and return
From another's eyes,
I, after so long,
Who have been wrong as you.

W. S. MERWIN

May 1506
    Christopher Columbus speaking:

I do not want your praises later on.
When I am dead I shall rest easier
In lack of borrowed breathing; and you will
Be tempted—never doubt—to sweeten up
Your own names with the fame of praising mine.
Even your scoffing mouths that so reviled me
Can learn again the shape of knew-him-when
And claim a talking share in India.

I began beggar and I finish beggared—
Beggared of gold and trumpets and renown
That Spain one moment lent me. It is nothing.
The unpaid tavern bill, the leaking roof
I would bequeath to later dangerous men
As their insurance of a happy death.

Feed on my bones if that will make you fat,
I can't prevent your feast; but all that marrow
Shall not fetch you memory of those beaches
And how they glittered beyond the tired sails.
Beggared I am but never of that look.
O rebels, traitors, slanderers, embezzlers

Who stole and lied to get me rags and chains!
I had my strength, but yours was cleverness;
Yet mine that troubles you the most, the longest.

God forgive me. Christ save the King and Queen
To whom I freely will all India.
I was no longer young when I first voyaged
And I was old and gutted at the last.

How did I harm you? Was my fame my crime?
Did my light, coruscant light of a new land
That was to shine for all, diminish yours?
Or did you think a feeding claw could hold it—
The gold—this side the King and the Word of God?
In that great wake beneath the foreign stars
What little Caesars sailed the charted course
And swarmed like eager spiders on the treasure
As though they could not wait to make it ruin—
That I had looked upon to name and bless.

Viceroy of India, Admiral of the Seas.
I wrap my names about me like old flags
That have had honor once, as well you know.
My grave has room for them and truth and me.
Cape Gracios à Dios and Veragua,
Andalusia's long way to Española,
Farthest-followed sun and under it
The curve of surf falling forward west.
Why did you hate my finding India?

WINFIELD TOWNLEY SCOTT

THE MEDITERRANEAN

*Quem das finem, rex magne, dolorum?**

Where we went in the boat was a long bay
A slingshot wide, walled in by towering stone—
Peaked margin of antiquity's delay,
And we went there out of time's monotone:

Where we went in the black hull no light moved
But a gull white-winged along the feckless wave,
The breeze, unseen but fierce as a body loved,
That boat drove onward like a willing slave:

Where we went in the small ship the seaweed
Parted and gave to us the murmuring shore,
And we made feast and in our secret need
Devoured the very plates Aeneas bore:

Where derelict you see through the low twilight
The green coast that you, thunder-tossed, would win,
Drop sail, and hastening to drink all night
Eat dish and bowl to take that sweet land in!

Where we feasted and caroused on the sandless
Pebbles, affecting our day of piracy,
What prophecy of eaten plates could landless
Wanderers fulfil by the ancient sea?

We for that time might taste the famous age
Eternal here yet hidden from our eyes
When lust of power undid its stuffless rage;
They, in a wineskin, bore earth's paradise.

---

*What end do you give of sorrows, great king?—H.P.

Let us lie down once more by the breathing side
Of Ocean, where our live forefathers sleep
As if the Known Sea still were a month wide—
Atlantis howls but is no longer steep!

What country shall we conquer, what fair land
Unman our conquest and locate our blood?
We've cracked the hemispheres with careless hand!
Now, from the Gates of Hercules we flood

Westward, westward till the barbarous brine
Whelms us to the tired land where tasseling corn,
Fat beans, grapes sweeter than muscadine
Rot on the vine: in that land were we born.

ALLEN TATE

COLUMBUS AND THE MERMAIDS

Off the coast of Hispaniola
off the strange coast, returning,
    the *Santa Maria* sighted three manatee,
sea cows holding their calves in their flippers
    above the water, suckling their young,
staring at the great sails
    and the high decks
and the ornate carvings of the *Santa Maria*
    with dark, round, unenlightened eyes.

And at the three manatee
    the Spaniards, saturated with wonders,
stared back, wondering still.
    Here were the sea women, the mermaids of whom men told,
the ones who combed their hair with golden combs,
    and sang ships to the rocks. Fishermen had caught
such in their nets and dragged them home
    weeping their pearl-like tears.
They had christened and even married them
    and begot children by them, children with green eyes.

Here were these wonders, yet like other wonders,
    once grappled, these seemed less than wonderful,
and that great dreamer, writing the ship's log,
    Columbus, thoughtful, turning the quill between
long fingers, meditating, frowning a little,
    possibly realizing that nothing is what it seems
(even islands, even continents), wrote of his mermaids:
    "They are not so beautiful as they are painted."

ELIZABETH COATSWORTH

AND OF COLUMBUS

Columbus is remembered by young men
who walk the world at night in street-walled prisons:
Where is my country? Why do I return
at midnight to a moonlit, inland ocean
whose waves beat as a heart beats in my side?

Is the return to these receding shores
the end of earth, fallen to deep-sea traffic,
the end of all things?

The cities that coil upward
from sumac bush and sand flow into grass:
roofs, towers mingle
with roots and the bodies of men who died
in foreign wars.

      Columbus who believed his own miracles,
conquered his India, oceans, mermaids, golden savages—
where was his country?

      It was a small stone room at night
in darkness. And time echoes time saying: Columbus no more,
where stars move toward the sun.

And in Havana under the Southern Cross, all that is his
is where his bones lie.

HORACE GREGORY

COLUMBUS

Inner greet.   Greenberg said it,
Even the tallest man needs inner greet.
This is the great word
brought back, in swinging seas.   The new world.

MURIEL RUKEYSER

Buffalo Dusk

✽ *INDIANS*

THE EAGLE'S SONG

Said the Eagle:
    I was astonished
    When I heard that there was death.

    My home, alas,
    Must I leave it!
    All beholding summits,
    Shall I see thee no more!

    North I went,
    Leaning on the wind;
    Through the forest resounded
    The cry of the hunted doe.

    East I went,
    Through the hot dawning;
    There was the smell of death in my nostrils.

    South I went, seeking
    The place where there is no death.
    Weeping I heard
    The voice of women
    Wailing for their children.

    West I went,
    On the world encompassing water;
    Death's trail was before me.

    People, O people,
    Needs be that we must die!

Therefore let us make
Songs together.
With a twine of songs to bind us
To the middle Heaven,
The white way of souls.
There we shall be at rest,
With our songs
We shall roam no more!

Southern California

MARY· AUSTIN

INABILITY TO DEPICT AN EAGLE

The eagles have practically left America.
Pouncing on an unexpected small creature,
Their talons fierce, they pick him to pieces.
Those great soaring wings that make us rejoice
Evantuate the male eagle to the top of a tall pine
From which he surveys illimitable ocean waters,
Flounces down on a lower abrasive nest; sated,
He reposes. He does not know that he has been poisoned.
Man the subtle, man the unknown, man the two-legged,
Has poisoned the food that feeds the bald eagles.

A psychic subtlety addresses the situation.
I have lost control of the bird as he has lost control
Of his subsistence. With an amazement bordering on devotion
I held before the movie lens the seven-foot wingspan
As the eagle took off and soared out over the ocean,
Made his powerful return to alight on the tallest pine,
Then drop to the rough nest. Alone. Was his mate killed
By the bullet of some ruthless American for sport?
Were his soarings looking for food, or for mate?
Is my self-consciousness more significant than his ignorance?

I held his heart in my telescopic lens with love,
I watched him in admiration in the tall summertime.
He was without equal. He was great in the skies in my eyes,
Only likened in majesty to some suffering poet
Who surveys the brutal headlands but is crushed to death
Almost before the realization of his scope,
Or like some voyager in the secrets of the soul
Who astounds us with the vitality of his presence
But who, like Socrates, is unknown in the market place,
Or like Christ, never tells us how it was on the Cross.

RICHARD EBERHART

MEMORIAL ODE

Chant

Now, listen, Ye who established the Great League,
Now it has become old,
Now there is nothing but wilderness.

Ye are in your graves who established it.
Ye have taken it with you and have placed it under you,
And there is nothing left but desert.
There you have taken your great minds.
That which you established, you have taken with you
Ye have placed under your heads what ye have established,
The Great League.

Refrain

Woe, woe! Hearken ye!
    We are diminished
Woe, woe!
    The land has become a thicket.
Woe, woe!
    The clear places are deserted
    They are in their graves who established it.
Woe, the Great League!
    Yet they declared it should endure.
The Great League, Woe!
    Their work has grown old
    We are become wretched. Woe!

CHIEF JOHN BUCK

Chief John Buck, hereditary Keeper of the Wampum, made and sang his ode in 1884 on the occasion of the removal of the bones of Chief Red Jacket from their original burying place to Forest Lawn Cemetery. The Great League is the League of the five Iroquois nations in Western New York. —George W. Cronyn, ed., *American Indian Poetry*

THE GRASS ON THE MOUNTAIN

Oh, long, long
The snow has possessed the mountains.

The deer have come down and the big-horn,
They have followed the Sun to the south
To feed on the mesquite pods and the bunch grass.
Loud are the thunder drums
In the tents of the mountains.

Oh, long, long
Have we eaten *chia* seeds
And dried deer's flesh of the summer killing.
We are wearied of our huts
And the smoky smell of our garments.

We are sick with desire of the sun
And the grass on the mountain.

From the Paiute

MARY AUSTIN

How busie are the sonnes of men?
How full their heads and hands?
What noyse and tumults in our owne,
    And eke in *Pagan* lands?

Yet I have found lesse noyse, more peace
    In wilde *America*,
Where women quickly build the house,
    And quickly move away.

English and *Indians* busie are,
    In parts of their abode:
Yet both stand *idle*, till God's call
    Set them to worke for God.

Mat. 20: 7*

Boast not proud *English*, of thy birth and blood,
    Thy brother *Indian* is by birth as Good.
Of one blood God made Him, and Thee and All,
    As wise, as faire, as strong, as personall.

By nature wrath's his portion, thine no more
    Till Grace *his* soule and *thine* in Christ restore
Make sure thy second birth, else thou shalt see,
    _Heaven ope to *Indians* wild, but shut to thee.

                              ROGER WILLIAMS

---

*They say unto him, Because no man hath hired us. He saith unto them, Go
ye also into the vineyard; and whatsoever is right, *that* shall ye receive.

THE END OF THE INDIAN POEMS

The pony air, wild wheat.
Sun the length of its shadow everywhere.
Montana, Dakota.

I want to lie down.
In the middle of the day, among
these stones, I want to go to sleep.

The snowtracks that lead out of my body,
the pony-prints, the wind
hovering the pale grass . . .

I don't want to walk in the circle
of a bird over bones,
the Hawk That Hunts Walking,

I don't want to walk in the circle
of my name
anymore. I know where I am.

I know the moon has my face on it,
I know the leaves tremble
like a tree of fish—

I know that winter
is a white country, but I want
to lie down.

I want to lie down here,
among stone and sunlight,
on the buffalo ground, anywhere.

STANLEY PLUMLY

19

LIKE GHOSTS OF EAGLES

The Indians have mostly gone
but not before they named the rivers
the rivers flow on
and the names of the rivers flow with them
    Susquehanna   Shenandoah

The rivers are now polluted plundered
but not the names of the rivers
cool and inviolate as ever
pure as on the morning of creation
    Tennessee   Tombigbee

If the rivers themselves should ever perish
I think the names will somehow somewhere hover
like ghosts of eagles
those mighty whisperers
    Missouri   Mississippi.

ROBERT FRANCIS

INDIAN NAMES

Ye say, they all have passed away,
  That noble race and brave;
That their light canoes have vanished
  From off the crested wave;
That, 'mid the forests where they roamed,
  There rings no hunter's shout;
But their name is on your waters,—
  Ye may not wash it out.

'Tis where Ontario's billow
  Like Ocean's surge is curled;
Where strong Niagara's thunders wake
  The echo of the world;
Where red Missouri bringeth
  Rich tribute from the West,
And Rappahannock sweetly sleeps
  On green Virginia's breast.

Ye say, their cone-like cabins,
  That clustered o'er the vale,
Have fled away, like withered leaves
  Before the Autumn gale;
But their memory liveth on your hills,
  Their baptism on your shore,
Your everlasting rivers speak
  Their dialect of yore.

Old Massachusetts wears it
  Within her lordly crown,
And broad Ohio bears it
  Amid his young renown;
Connecticut hath wreathed it
  Where her quiet foliage waves,
And bold Kentucky breathes it hoarse
  Through all her ancient caves.

Wachuset hides its lingering voice
  Within its rocky heart.
And Alleghany graves its tone
  Throughout his lofty chart;
Monadnock, on his forehead hoar,
  Doth seal the sacred trust;
Your mountains build their monument,
  Though ye destroy their dust.

LYDIA HUNTLY SIGOURNEY

HANDS

Inside a cave in a narrow canyon near Tassajara
The vault of rock is painted with hands,
A multitude of hands in the twilight, a cloud of men's palms,
  no more,
No other picture. There's no one to say
Whether the brown shy quiet people who are dead intended
Religion or magic, or made their tracings
In the idleness of art; but over the division of years these
  careful
Signs-manual are now like a sealed message
Saying: "Look: we also were human; we had hands, not paws.
  All hail
You people with the cleverer hands, our supplanters
In the beautiful country; enjoy her a season, her beauty and
  come down
And be supplanted; for you also are human."

ROBINSON JEFFERS

SONG OF SITTING BULL

A warrior
  I have been;
  now
  it is all over.
A hard time
  I have.

UNREAL THE BUFFALO IS STANDING

He said, unreal the buffalo is standing.
These are his sayings,
    unreal the buffalo is standing,
    unreal he stands in the open space,
    unreal he is standing.

IT IS MINE, THIS COUNTRY WIDE

Yonder they are coming.
Although strange misfortunes have befallen me,
    yet it is mine, this country wide.

From *American Indian Poetry*, George W. Cronyn, ed.

THE PROPHECY OF KING TAMMANY

The Indian chief who, fam'd of yore,
Saw Europe's sons advent'ring here,
Look'd sorrowing to the crowded shore,
    And sighing dropt a tear!
He saw them half his world explore,
He saw them draw the shining blade,
He saw their hostile ranks display'd,
And cannons blazing through that shade
    Where only peace was known before.

"Ah, what unequal arms!" he cry'd,
"How art thou fallen, my country's pride,
    The rural, sylvan reign!
Far from our pleasing shores to go
To western rivers, winding slow,
Is this the boon the gods bestow!
    What have we done, great patrons, say,
    That strangers seize our woods away,
        And drive us naked from our native plain.

Rage and revenge inspire my soul,
And passion burns without controul;
    Hence, strangers, to your native shore!
Far from our Indian shades retire,
Remove these *gods* that vomit fire,
    And stain with blood these ravag'd glades no more.

Tammany was an Indian chief in the Delaware Valley in 1654. He advocated friendship with the colonists and became a symbol of American resistance to tyranny. The Society of Tammany was founded in New York in 1786.
    Philip Freneau (1752-1832) was an influential editor and poet, and an ardent advocate of Jeffersonian democracy.—H.P.

In vain I weep, in vain I sigh,
These strangers all our arms defy,
As they advance our chieftains die!—
    What can their hosts oppose!

The bow has lost its wonted spring,
The arrow faulters on the wing,
Nor carries ruin from the string
    To end their being and our woes.

Yes, yes,—I see our nation bends;
The gods no longer are our friends,
    But why these weak complaints and sighs?
Are there not gardens in the west,
Where all our far fam'd Sachems rest?—
I'll go, an unexpected guest,
    And the dark horrors of the way despise.

Ev'n now the thundering peal draws nigh,
'Tis theirs to triumph, ours to die!
But mark me, Christian, ere I go—
Thou, too, shalt have thy share of woe,
The time rolls on, not moving slow,
When hostile squadrons for your blood shall come
    And ravage all your shore!
Your warriors and your children slay,
And some in dismal dungeons lay,
Or lead them captive far away,
    To climes unknown, thro' seas untry'd before.

When struggling long, at last with pain
You break a cruel tyrant's chain,
That never shall be join'd again,
    When half your foes are homeward fled,
    And hosts on hosts in triumph led,
    And hundreds maim'd and thousands dead,
    A timid race shall then succeed,
        Shall slight the virtues of the firmer race,
        That brought your tyrant to disgrace,
Shall give your honours to an odious train,
Who shunn'd all conflicts on the main
And dar'd no battles on the bloody plain,
Whose little souls sunk in the gloomy day
When VIRTUE ONLY could support the fray
And sunshine friends kept off—or ran away."

So spoke the chief, and rais'd his funeral pyre—
    Around him soon the crackling flames ascend;
He smil'd amid the fervours of the fire
    To think his troubles were so near their end,
Till the freed soul, her debt to nature paid,
Rose from the ashes that her prison made,
And sought the world unknown, and dark oblivion's shade.

PHILIP FRENEAU

from *THE SONG OF HIAWATHA*

From his wanderings far to eastward,
From the regions of the morning,
From the shining land of Wabun,
Homeward now returned Iagoo,
The great traveller, the great boaster,
Full of new and strange adventures,
Marvels many and many wonders.
    And the people of the village
Listened to him as he told them
Of his marvellous adventures,
Laughing answered him in this wise:
"Ugh! it is indeed Iagoo!
No one else beholds such wonders!"
    He had seen, he said, a water
Bigger than the Big-Sea-Water,
Broader than the Gitche Gumee,
Bitter so that none could drink it!
At each other looked the warriors,
Looked the women at each other,
Smiled, and said, "It cannot be so!
Kaw!" they said, "it cannot be so!"
    O'er it, said he, o'er this water
Came a great canoe with pinions,
A canoe with wings came flying,
Bigger than a grove of pine-trees,
Taller than the tallest tree-tops!
And the old men and the women
Looked and tittered at each other;
"Kaw!" they said, "we don't believe it!"
    From its mouth, he said, to greet him,
Came Waywassimo, the lightning,
Came the thunder, Annemeekee!

And the warriors and the women
Laughed aloud at poor Iagoo;
"Kaw!" they said, "what tales you tell us!"
    In it, said he, came a people,
In the great canoe with pinions
Came, he said, a hundred warriors;
Painted white were all their faces
And with hair their chins were covered!
And the warriors and the women
Laughed and shouted in derision,
Like the ravens on the tree-tops,
Like the crows upon the hemlocks.
"Kaw!" they said, "what lies you tell us!
Do not think that we believe them!"
    Only Hiawatha laughed not,
But he gravely spake and answered
To their jeering and their jesting:
"True is all Iagoo tells us;
I have seen it in a vision,
Seen the great canoe with pinions,
Seen the people with white faces,
Seen the coming of this bearded
People of the wooden vessel
From the regions of the morning,
From the shining land of Wabun.
    "Gitche Manito, the Mighty,
The Great Spirit, the Creator,
Sends them hither on his errand.
Sends them to us with his message.
Wheresoe'er they move, before them
Swarms the stinging fly, the Ahmo,
Swarms the bee, the honey-maker;
Wheresoe'er they tread, beneath them
Springs a flower unknown among us,
Springs the White-man's Foot in blossom.

❦ *29*

"Let us welcome, then, the strangers,
Hail them as our friends and brothers,
And the heart's right hand of friendship
Give them when they come to see us.
Gitche Manito, the Mighty,
Said this to me in my vision.

    "I beheld, too, in that vision
All the secrets of the future,
Of the distant days that shall be.
I beheld the westward marches
Of the unknown, crowded nations.
All the land was full of people,
Restless, struggling, toiling, striving,
Speaking many tongues, yet feeling
But one heart-beat in their bosoms.
In the woodlands rang their axes,
Smoked their towns in all the valleys,
Over all the lakes and rivers
Rushed their great canoes of thunder.

    "Then a darker, drearier vision
Passed before me, vague and cloud-like;
I beheld our nation scattered,
All forgetful of my counsels,
Weakened, warring with each other:
Saw the remnants of our people
Sweeping westward, wild and woful,
Like the cloud-rack of a tempest,
Like the withered leaves of Autumn!"

HENRY WADSWORTH LONGFELLOW

NEW MEXICAN MOUNTAIN

I watch the Indians dancing to help the young corn at Taos
  pueblo. The old men squat in a ring
And make the song, the young women with fat bare arms,
  and a few shame-faced young men, shuffle the dance.

The lean-muscled men are naked to the narrow loins,
  their breasts and backs daubed with white clay,
Two eagle-feathers plume the black heads. They dance with
  reluctance, they are growing civilized; the old men
  persuade them.

Only the drum is confident, it thinks the world has not
  changed; the beating heart, the simplest of rhythms,
It thinks the world has not changed at all; it is only a dreamer,
  a brainless heart, the drum has no eyes.

These tourists have eyes, the hundred watching the dance,
  white Americans, hungrily too, with reverence, not
  laughter;
Pilgrims from civilization, anxiously seeking beauty, religion,
  poetry; pilgrims from the vacuum.

People from cities, anxious to be human again. Poor show how
  they suck you empty! The Indians are emptied,
And certainly there was never religion enough, nor beauty
  nor poetry here . . . to fill Americans.

Only the drum is confident, it thinks the world has not
  changed. Apparently only myself and the strong
Tribal drum, and the rockhead of Taos mountain, remember
  that civilization is a transient sickness.

ROBINSON JEFFERS

BUFFALO DUSK

The buffaloes are gone.
　And those who saw the buffaloes are gone.
Those who saw the buffaloes by thousands and how they
　pawed the prairie sod into dust with their hoofs, their great
　heads down pawing on in a great pageant of dusk,
Those who saw the buffaloes are gone.
And the buffaloes are gone.

CARL SANDBURG

ARROWY DREAMS

We had red earth once to smear on our cheeks
And our arrows were made of mountain peaks
For buffalo that still go by
Cloudy in the evening sky.
But now we must open colored cans
To eat from the store like the pale-face clans —
Except when we pick a goat from the hill
Or a rabbit races and is still—
Or a buffalo plunges his head and steams
Through our swift-hooved, ancient, arrowy dreams.

WITTER BYNNER

INSCRIPTION

*For the bas-relief by Preston Powers, carved upon the
huge boulder in Denver Park, Col., and representing the
Last Indian and the Last Bison.*

The eagle, stooping from yon snow-blown peaks,
For the wild hunter and the bison seeks,
In the changed world below; and finds alone
Their graven semblance in the eternal stone.

JOHN GREENLEAF WHITTIER

The Westwardness
of Everything

❈ *SETTLERS*

IMMIGRANTS

No ship of all that under sail or steam
Have gathered people to us more and more
But, Pilgrim-manned, the *Mayflower* in a dream
Has been her anxious convoy in to shore.

ROBERT FROST

TO THE WESTERN WORLD

A siren sang, and Europe turned away
From the high castle and the shepherd's crook.
Three caravels went sailing to Cathay
On the strange ocean, and the captains shook
Their banners out across the Mexique Bay.

And in our early days we did the same.
Remembering our fathers in their wreck
We crossed the sea from Palos where they came
And saw, enormous to the little deck,
A shore in silence waiting for a name.

The treasures of Cathay were never found.
In this America, this wilderness
Where the axe echoes with a lonely sound,
The generations labor to possess
And grave by grave we civilize the ground.

LOUIS SIMPSON

JAMESTOWN

Let me look at what I was, before I die.
Strange, that one's photograph in kindergarten
Is a captain in a ruff and a Venusian
—Is nothing here American?
John Smith is squashed
Beneath the breasts of Pocahontas: some true Christian,
Engraving all, has made the captain Man,
The maiden the most voluptuous of newts.
Met in a wood and lain with, this red demon,
The mother of us all, lies lovingly
Upon the breastplate of our father: the First Family
Of Jamestown trembles beneath the stone
Axe—then Powhatan, smiling, gives the pair his blessing
And nymphs and satyrs foot it at their wedding.
The continents, like country children, peep in awe
As Power, golden as a Veronese,
Showers her riches on the lovers: Nature,
Nature at last is married to a man.

The two lived happily
Forever after. . . . And I only am escaped alone
To tell the story. But how shall I tell the story?
The settlers died? All settlers die. The colony
Was a Lost Colony? All colonies are lost.
John Smith and Pocahontas, carving on a tree
We Have Gone Back For More People, crossed the sea
And were put to death, for treason, in the Tower
Of London? Ah, but they needed no one!

Powhatan,
Smiling at that red witch, red wraith, his daughter,
Said to the father of us all, John Smith:
"American,
To thyself be enough! . . ." He was enough—
Enough, or too much. The True Historie
Of the Colony of Jamestown is a wish.

Long ago, hundreds of years ago, a man
Met a woman in a wood, a witch.
The witch said, "Wish!"
The man said, "Make me what I am."
The witch said, "Wish again!"
The man said, "Make me what I am."
The witch said, "For the last time, wish!"
The man said, "Make me what I am."
The witch said: "Mortal, because you have believed
In your mortality, there is no wood, no wish,
No world, there is only you. But what are you?
The world has become you. But what are you?
Ask;
Ask, while the time to ask remains to you."

The witch said, smiling: "This is Jamestown.
From Jamestown, Virginia, to Washington, D.C.,
Is, as the rocket flies, eleven minutes."

RANDALL JARRELL

from GOOD NEWS FROM NEW ENGLAND

Of the arrivall of our English Nation at the
Mattachusets Bay, &c

With hearts revived in conceit, new land and trees they eye,
    Senting the Caedars and sweet ferne from heats reflection
      drye,
Much like the bird from dolsome Romes inclos'd in cage of
    wyre,
    Set forth in fragrant fields doth skip in hope of her desire.
So leap the hearts of these mixt men by streights o're seas
    inured,
    To following hard-ships wildernesse, doth force to be
      endured.
In clipping armes of out-strecht Capes, there ships now gliding
    enter,
    In bay where many little Isles do stand in waters Center.
Where Sea-calves with their hairy heads gaze 'bove the waters
    brim,
    Wondering to see such uncouth sights their sporting place
    to swim.
The seas vast length makes welcome shores unto this wandring
    race,
    Who now found footing freely for, Christs Church his
    resting place.

EDWARD JOHNSON

Edward Johnson came to America in 1630 with Governor John Winthrop.—
H.P.

UPPON THE FIRST SIGHT
OF NEW-ENGLAND
JUNE 29, 1638

Hayle holy-land wherein our holy lord
Hath planted his most true and holy word
Hayle happye people who have dispossest
Your selves of friends, and meanes, to find some rest
For your poore wearied soules, opprest of late
For Jesus-sake, with Envye, spight, and hate
To yow that blessed promise truly's given   *Math.* 19: 29*
Of sure reward, which you'l receve in heaven
Methinks I heare the Lambe of God thus speake
Come my deare little flocke, who for my sake
Have lefte your Country, dearest friends, and goods
And hazarded your lives o'th raginge floods
Posses this Country; free from all anoye
Heare I'le bee with you, heare you shall Injoye
My sabbaths, sacraments, my minestrye
And ordinances in their puritye

Thomas Tillam was not the only traveler to America in the early seventeenth century to feel a sense of dedication mixed with wonder as he viewed the land that was to be shaped into the modern Canaan. But none other recorded his response in lines so unmistakably inspired and genuinely lyrical.

For reasons not altogether clear—perhaps disillusionment at the rigidity of religious controls exercised in New England . . . Tillam did not remain long in America.—Harrison T. Meserole, *Seventeenth-Century American Poetry*

*And every one that hath forsaken houses, or brethren, or sisters, or father, or mother, or wife, or children, or lands, for my name's sake, shall receive an hundredfold, and shall inherit everlasting life.

But yet beware of Sathans wylye baites
Hee lurkes amongs yow, Cunningly hee waites
To Catch yow from mee; live not then secure
But fight 'gainst sinne, and let your lives be pure
Prepare to heare your sentence thus expressed
Come yee my servants of my father Blessed   *Math.* 25: 34†

THOMAS TILLAM

†Then shall the King say unto them on his right hand, Come, ye blessed of my
Father, inherit the kingdom prepared for you from the foundation of the
world.

Driving through New England
by broken barns and pastures
i long for the rains of Wydah
and the gardens
ripe as history
oranges and citron
limefruit and African apple
not just this springtime and
these wheatfields
white poets call the past.

LUCILLE CLIFTON

ON BEING BROUGHT FROM AFRICA TO AMERICA

Twas mercy brought me from my Pagan land,
Taught my benighted soul to understand
That there's a God, that there's a Saviour too.
Once I redemption neither sought nor knew.
Some view our sable race with scornful eye;
"Their colour is a diabolic dye."
Remember, Christians, Negroes, black as Cain,
May be refined, and join the angelic train.

PHILLIS WHEATLEY

Phillis Wheatley, born in Africa in 1753, was sold to the John Wheatley family, who taught her to read and write. She became a famous poet in her own time. In 1778 she was given her freedom.—H.P.

ARRIVAL, NEW YORK HARBOR

Last night we anchored in
a fog. This morning
the fog lifted:
a miniscule town
scattered along the wide
curving harbor. Boats and
ships of every description
rocking at anchor.

My mind has dwelt perpetually
on the vast forests beyond
this harbor, where we must go.
The trees are wings waiting
to greet us. The trees are
thirsty for our arrival. All
around the Niskeyuna tract
angels have set flares. Zion
is a step away! Zion!

ROBERT PETERS

Mother Ann Lee, the founder of the Shaker sect, came to America on
August 6, 1774, in search of religious freedom. The simple, beautiful furni-
ture built by her followers may be seen in many American museums.

Oh! dearer by far than the land of our birth
  Is the land where the hours of our infancy flew
And the dearest and loveliest spot upon earth
  Is the spot where our loves and affections first grew.

What home can we have but the home of the heart
  What country but that of our friends can we claim
Or where is the powerful spell that can part
  The soul from the scenes of its hopes and its fame?

Then tell us no more we were born far away
  Where Liberty's star never rose or has set
We were nursed where it shines and have caught from its ray
  A warmth which our bosoms can never forget!

And dearer by far than the land of our birth
  Is the land where the hours of our infancy flew
And the dearest and loveliest spot upon earth
  Is the spot where our loves and affections first grew!

RICHARD HENRY WILDE

OUR STARS COME FROM IRELAND

I

Tom McGreevy, in America,
Thinks of Himself as a Boy

Out of him that I loved,
Mal Bay I made,
I made Mal Bay
And him in that water.

Over the top of the Bank of Ireland,
The wind blows quaintly
Its thin-stringed music,
As he heard it in Tarbert.

These things were made of him
And out of myself.
He stayed in Kerry, died there.
I live in Pennsylvania.

Out of him I made Mal Bay
And not a bald and tasselled saint.
What would the water have been,
Without that that he makes of it?

The stars are washing up from Ireland
And through and over the puddles of Swatara
And Schuylkill. The sound of him
Comes from a great distance and is heard.

The Westwardness of Everything

These are the ashes of fiery weather,
Of nights full of the green stars from Ireland,
Wet out of the sea, and luminously wet,
Like beautiful and abandoned refugees.

The whole habit of the mind is changed by them,
These Gaeled and fitful-fangled darknesses
Made suddenly luminous, themselves a change,
An east in their compelling westwardness,

Themselves an issue as at an end, as if
There was an end at which in a final change,
When the whole habit of the mind was changed,
The ocean breathed out morning in one breath.

WALLACE STEVENS

STANZAS ON THE EMIGRATION
TO AMERICA, AND PEOPLING
THE WESTERN COUNTRY

[*1785*]

To western woods, and lonely plains,
Palemon from the crowd departs,
Where nature's wildest genius reigns,
To tame the soil, and plant the arts—
    What wonders there shall freedom show,
    What mighty *States* successive grow!

From Europe's proud, despotic shores
Hither the stranger takes his way,
And in our new found world explores
A happier soil, a milder sway,
    Where no proud despot holds him down,
    No slaves insult him with a crown.

What charming scenes attract the eye,
On wild Ohio's savage stream!
Here nature reigns, whose works outvie
The boldest pattern art can frame;
    Here ages past have roll'd away,
    And forests bloom'd—but to decay.

From these fair plains, these rural seats,
So long conceal'd, so lately known,
The unsocial Indian far retreats,
To make some other clime his own,
    Where other streams, less pleasing, flow,
    And darker forests round him grow.

Great Sire of floods! whose varied wave
Through climes and countries takes its way,*
To whom creating nature gave
Ten thousand streams to swell thy sway!
   No longer shall *they* useless prove,
   Nor idly through the forests rove;

Nor shall the voice of war molest,
Nor Europe's all-aspiring pride—
   Here reason shall new laws devise,
   And order from confusion rise.

Forsaking kings and regal state,
(A debt that reason deems amiss)
The traveller owns, convinc'd though late,
No realm so free, so blest as this—
   The *east* is half to slaves consign'd,
   And half to slavery more refin'd.

O come the time, and haste the day,
When man shall man no longer crush,
When reason shall enforce her sway,
Nor these fair regions raise our blush,
   Where still the African complains,
   And mourns his yet unbroken chains.

Far brighter scenes, a future age,
The muse predicts, these States shall hail,
Whose genius shall the world engage,
Whose deeds shall over death prevail,
   And happier systems bring to view
   Than all the eastern sages knew.

---

*Mississippi River

Nor longer shall the princely flood
From distant lakes be swell'd in vain,
Nor longer through a darksome wood
Advance, unnotic'd, to the main,
    Far other ends the fates decree—
    And commerce plans new freights for thee.

While virtue warms the generous breast,
Here heaven-born freedom shall reside,
Nor shall the voice of war molest,
Nor Europe's all-aspiring pride—
    Here reason shall new laws devise,
    And order from confusion rise.

PHILIP FRENEAU

REFUGEE IN AMERICA

There are words like *Freedom*
Sweet and wonderful to say.
On my heart-strings freedom sings
All day everyday.

There are words like *Liberty*
That almost make me cry.
If you had known what I knew
You would know why.

LANGSTON HUGHES

WOMEN

They were women then
My mama's generation
Husky of voice—Stout of
Step
With fists as well as
Hands
How they battered down
Doors
And ironed
Starched white
Shirts
How they led
Armies
Headragged Generals
Across mined
Fields
Booby-trapped
Ditches
To discover books
Desks
A place for us
How they knew what we
Must know
Without knowing a page
Of it
Themselves.

ALICE WALKER

54

BURYING GROUND BY THE TIES

Ayee! Ai! This is heavy earth on our shoulders:
There were none of us born to be buried in this earth:
Niggers we were, Portuguese, Magyars, Polacks:

We were born to another look of the sky certainly.
Now we lie here in the river pastures:
We lie in the mowings under the thick turf:

We hear the earth and the all-day rasp of the grasshoppers.
It was we laid the steel to this land from ocean to ocean:
It was we (if you know) put the U.P. through the passes

Bringing her down into Laramie full load,
Eighteen mile on the granite anticlinal,
Forty-three foot to the mile and the grade holding:

It was we did it: hunkies of our kind.
It was we dug the caved-in holes for the cold water:
It was we built the gully spurs and the freight sidings:

Who would do it but we and the Irishmen bossing us?
It was all foreign-born men there were in this country:
It was Scotsmen, Englishmen, Chinese, Squareheads,
    Austrians . . .

Ayee! but there's weight to the earth under it.
Not for this did we come out—to be lying here
Nameless under the ties in the clay cuts:

There's nothing good in the world but the rich will buy it:
Everything sticks to the grease of a gold note—
Even a continent—even a new sky!

Do not pity us much for the strange grass over us:
We laid the steel to the stone stock of these mountains:
The place of our graves is marked by the telegraph poles!

It was not to lie in the bottoms we came out
And the trains going over us here in the dry hollows ...

ARCHIBALD MAC LEISH

THE TRAIL INTO KANSAS

The early wagons left no sign
no smoke betrays them
line pressed in the grass *we were here*
all night the sun bleeds in us
and the wound slows us in the daytime
will it heal
there

we few
late
we gave our names to each other to keep
wrapped in their old bells
the wrappings work loose
something eats them when we sleep and wakes us
ringing

when day comes
shadows that were once ours and came back to look
stand up for a moment ahead of us
and then vanish
we know we are
watched but there is no danger
nothing that lives waits for us
nothing is eternal

we have been guided from scattered wombs
all the way here choosing choosing
which foot to put down
we are like wells moving
over the prairie
a blindness a hollow a cold source
will any be happy to see us
in the new home

W. S. MERWIN

ADDRESS TO THE REFUGEES

We have the statue for it—Liberty,
Whose classic vulgar hands invite you Home,
Whatever future storms your reverie

Upon the lank Atlantic waste, come,
Dissolve the terror and suspend the night;
Let every dragon for a little while be dumb.

We, too, have tasted whips and salt, the weight
Of willful ignorance; drilled on our eyes,
Have felt, somehow, the acrid headlines cut

Brands of outraged innocence across
Your unmoved mouths. Without a foreign gift,
Bereft of anything but prophecies

To place intrepidly upon our soft,
Unbludgeoned palms, come into this, our day;
Where promises, at least, are someway left,

Where Love, perhaps, may find its ultimate way,
Since we are young, and all our documents
Have not submitted and will not betray.

JOHN MALCOLM BRINNIN

TO THE STATUE

The square-heeled boat sets off for the Statue.
People are stuck up tight as asparagus stalks
inside the red rails (ribbons tying the bunch.)

The tips, their rigid heads against the fog,
all yearn toward the Statue; dents of waves
all minimize and multiply to where

she, fifteen minutes afar (a cooky-tin-shaped-
mother-doll) stands without a feature
except her little club of flame.

Other boats pass the promenade. It's exciting
to watch the water heave up, clop the pier,
and even off: a large unsteady belly,

oil-scaled, gasping, then breathing normally.
On the curved horizon, faded shapes of ships,
with thready regalia, cobweb a thick sky.

Nearer, a spluttering bubble over the water
(a mosquito's skeletal hindpart, wings detached
and fused to whip on top like a child's whirltoy)

holds two policemen. They're seated in the air,
serge, brass-buttoned paunches behind glass,
serene, on rubber runners, sledding fog.

Coming back, framed by swollen pilings,
the boat is only inches wide, and flat.
Stalk by stalk, they've climbed into her head

(its bronze is green out there, and hugely spiked)
and down her winding spine into their package,
that now bobs forward on the water's mat.

Soon three-dimensional, colored like a drum,
red-staved, flying a dotted flag,
its rusty iron toe divides the harbor;
sparkling shavings curl out from the bow.
Their heads have faces now. They've been to the Statue.
She has no face from here, but just a fist.
(The flame is carved like an asparagus tip.)

MAY SWENSON

PROSPECTIVE IMMIGRANTS
PLEASE NOTE

Either you will
go through this door
or you will not go through.

If you go through
there is always the risk
of remembering your name.

Things look at you doubly
and you must look back
and let them happen.

If you do not go through
it is possible
to live worthily

to maintain your attitudes
to hold your position
to die bravely

but much will blind you,
much will evade you,
at what cost who knows?

The door itself
makes no promises.
It is only a door.

ADRIENNE RICH

ELEGY FOR BELLA, SARAH, ROSIE, AND ALL THE OTHERS

They're dying off, the kerchiefed
women from central Europe
who followed their men, jammed
between rotting staves of freighters.

Stones placed on their headstones
show our esteem, not for their blind
cotton courage, tied under their chins,
hiding the half-choked throat,

not to keep off marauders,
as we did once in the desert,
but stones to show we honor their histories
which we cried out against
when they still trafficked in strudel.

They're burying you one by one,
my mothers from Romania, Poland,
and the Carpathians. We swarm
over the gravegrass with memories of you
melting in our mouths like good pastry.

Oh my pearls beyond price, goodbye
from your liberated American daughter,
whose tears, the color of martinis,
drop by drop grow cold
on the invisible thread.

SONYA DORMAN

OF BEING NUMEROUS #24

In this nation
Which is in some sense
Our home. Covenant!

The covenant is:
There shall be peoples.

GEORGE OPPEN

I have fallen in love
with American names

❧❧ *REGIONS*

NIGHT JOURNEY

Now as the train bears west,
Its rhythm rocks the earth,
And from my Pullman berth
I stare into the night
While others take their rest.
Bridges of iron lace,
A suddenness of trees,
A lap of mountain mist
All cross my line of sight,
Then a bleak wasted place,
And a lake below my knees.
Full on my neck I feel
The straining at a curve;
My muscles move with steel,
I wake in every nerve.
I watch a beacon swing
From dark to blazing bright;
We thunder through ravines
And gullies washed with light.
Beyond the mountain pass
Mist deepens on the pane;
We rush into a rain
That rattles double glass.
Wheels shake the roadbed stone,
The pistons jerk and shove,
I stay up half the night
To see the land I love.

THEODORE ROETHKE

N.Y. TO L.A. BY JET PLANE

Retired gardener of solitudes,
this clear noon I put wings
on my wheelbarrow, ready for the plains,
color of puma and Indian.
   By Cleveland I've forgotten the terrors
   of acceleration as we pour up
   over greens and granites.
Sunlight roars off the port wing
which burns like a sword. I sit
on the Grand Canyon side wishing to ride
a burro down into that worm of darkness
wound through the heart of the continent.
   The Rockies feed me fierce dreams
   of a cold camp and ice water
   bursting out.
   O Moses, what a promised land.
Here's the desert, burnt, flat,
tawny as a cougar, mountains forging
its border. I want to ride
a clever pony through the passes
before billboards start stalking us.
   From the heights I thunder, one leg
   in my north Atlantic, one knee-deep
   in the wild lilac of the Pacific Palisades.
Maybe when I die, my ghost on jet wings
will be ferried across the country forever.

SONYA DORMAN

OUR COUNTRY

It is a noble country where we dwell,
Fit for a stalwart race to summer in;
From Madawaska to Red River raft,
From Florid keys to the Missouri forks,
See what unwearied (and) copious streams
Come tumbling to the east and southern shore,
To find a man stand on their lowland banks:
Behold the innumerous rivers and the licks
Where he may drink to quench his summer's thirst,
And the broad corn and rice fields yonder, where
His hands may gather for his winter's store.

See the fair reaches of the northern lakes
To cool his summer with their inland breeze,
And the long slumbering Appalachian range
Offering its slopes to his unwearied knees!
See what a long-lipped sea doth clip the shores,
And noble strands where navies may find port;
See Boston, Baltimore, and New York stand
Fair in the sunshine on the eastern sea,
And yonder too the fair green prairie.

See the red race with sullen step retreat,
Emptying its graves, striking the wigwam tent,
And where the rude camps of its brethren stand,
Dotting the distant green, their herds around;
In serried ranks, and with a distant clang,
Their fowl fly o'er, bound to the northern lakes,
Whose plashing waves invite their webbéd feet.

Such the fair reach and prospect of the land,
The journeying summer creeps from south to north
With wearied feet, resting in many a vale;
Its length doth tire the seasons to o'ercome,
Its widening breadth doth make the sea-breeze pause
And spend its breath against the mountain's side:
Still serene Summer paints the southern fields,
While the stern Winter reigns on northern hills.

Look nearer,—know the lineaments of each face,—
Learn the far-travelled race, and find here met
The so long gathering congress of the world!
The Afric race brought here to curse its fate,
Erin to bless,—the patient German too,
Th' industrious Swiss, the fickle, sanguine Gaul,
And manly Saxon, leading all the rest.
All things invite this earth's inhabitants
To rear their lives to an unheard-of height,
And meet the expectation of the land;
To give at length the restless race of man
A pause in the long westering caravan.

HENRY DAVID THOREAU

CROSSING

STOP   LOOK   LISTEN
as gate stripes swing down,
count the cars hauling distance
upgrade through town:
warning whistle, bellclang,
engine eating steam,
engineer waving,
a fast-freight dream:
B&M boxcar,
boxcar again,
Frisco gondola,
eight-nine-ten,
Erie and Wabash,
Seaboard, U.P.,
Pennsy tankcar,
twenty-two, three,
Phoebe Snow, B&O,
thirty-four, five,
Santa Fe cattle
shipped alive,
red cars, yellow cars,
orange cars, black,
Youngstown steel
down to Mobile
on Rock Island track,
fifty-nine, sixty,
hoppers of coke,
Anaconda copper,
hotbox smoke,

eighty-eight,
red-ball freight,
Rio Grande,
Nickel Plate,
Hiawatha,
Lackawanna,
rolling fast
and loose,
ninety-seven,
coal car,
boxcar,
CABOOSE!

PHILIP BOOTH

AN ENGLISHMAN WITH AN ATLAS
or
AMERICA THE UNPRONOUNCEABLE

How sweet, to see the dells so shady
   That fancy summons up afar
In green-and-gold Schenectady
   And the dim glades of Wilkes-Barre!

How fortunate would be the poet
   Who bids his tuneful numbers flow
To sing the praises of Detroit
   And many-peopled Toledo!

Into the west, through meadows flowery,
   Happily would he take his way
To see the sparkling-blue Missouri
   And greet the French of Joliet,

And watch the sloe-eyed señorita
   Smile at her cavalier's "holá!"
In the bright plazas of Wichita,
   The patios of Topeka;

And west, like arrowy bird or beetle,
   Till the submerging sun reveals
The shimmering pinnacles of Seattle,
   The heavenly city, Los Angeles!

MORRIS BISHOP

NEW ENGLAND

Here where the wind is always north-north-east
And children learn to walk on frozen toes,
Wonder begets an envy of all those
Who boil elsewhere with such a lyric yeast
Of love that you will hear them at a feast
Where demons would appeal for some repose,
Still clamoring where the chalice overflows
And crying wildest who have drunk the least.

Passion is here a soilure of the wits,
We're told, and Love a cross for them to bear;
Joy shivers in the corner where she knits
And Conscience always has the rocking-chair,
Cheerful as when she tortured into fits
The first cat that was ever killed by Care.

EDWIN ARLINGTON ROBINSON

THE MEN OF SUDBURY

(For and after H. D. Thoreau)

Greater, he called them, than Homer or Chaucer or
   Shakespeare,
Fuller of talk than a chestnut is of its meat,
Keeping their castles or chopping alone in the woodlots;

Moving at morning through fields with their long ducking
   guns,
Wading with watertight boots in the fowl-meadow grass,
Hunting the teal and the ospreys, the black ducks and
   whistlers;

Men who were rude and sturdy, experienced and wise,
Clearing and burning and scratching the face of the earth,
Subsoiling, harrowing, plowing, again and again;

Only they never found time to set it all down;
They were never men who took to the way of writing:
Outdoors they were, outdoors every day of their lives.

Greater, he said, than Shakespeare or Chaucer or Homer.
But he was one who took to the way of writing.
The men of Sudbury move now in his pages.

CARLOS BAKER

A NEW ENGLAND SAMPLER

Miss Dickinson is gone;
Mr. Thoreau has lain
In deeper Concord for
Some three-score years and more.
I had thought these were bones
Would rise like tawny pines.

Cabot came down this way,
Took five redskins away
To show for sixpence in
Alleys Shakespearian.
I had thought these were bones
Would rise like tawny pines.

Newport, when Henry James
Was there, smelled of the Thames;
His polished jaw and eye
Furthered the heresy.
I had thought these were bones
Would rise like tawny pines.

When Jonathan Edwards went
To live in a Berkshire tent,
The Indians knew the result:
His tongue was difficult.
I had thought these were bones
Would rise like tawny pines.

Scholarship and time
Have brought them bookish fame,
Whose biographies on stone
Are paged by the careless rain.
I had thought these were bones
Would rise like tawny pines.

JOHN MALCOLM BRINNIN

AMERICAN PLAN

The antique Indian should be Henry James
   Notebook in hand, a well-disguised impostor;
The porch should (spiritually) face the Thames
   And not the Vineyard or East Gloucester.

The juke-box in the Palm Court should play Herbert
   For ladies quite exhausted from croquet;
The chocolate popsicle should be lime sherbet
   Served in a glass on a hand-painted tray.

The man in the Hawaiian wrap-around
   Should wear white flannels and a State St. boater;
His wife on water-skis across the Sound
   Should make her bread-and-butter calls by motor.

His daughter in the slacks should loll and dally
   Under a parasol from *Maison Worth*;
The things her mad-cap girl-chums say should really
   Put her in stitches, into gales of mirth.

The Chris-Craft should be an Old Town Canoe;
   The yellow Jeepster in the *porte cochere*
Should be a Willys-Overland tonneau,
   Equipped with robes, ferns, curtains and a spare.

When rats desert a bather's hair-do, all
   Well-meaning sympathy should quite unnerve her;
To thwart the masher and the ne'er-do-well,
   The bathing dress should be a life-preserver.

Photographers with tripod, hood and birdie,
   Should take group-portraits on the tennis lawn;
The families should look joyless, drawn, but sturdy:
   Men standing, women seated, children prone.

From cupola and minaret should fly
   The flags of summertime, old and windswept.
("Gay Whirl at Ocean House" reported by
   The New York Herald and *The Boston Transcript*.)

For jolly times that should be had by all,
   For moonlight sings, for roundelay and ballad,
The picnic launch should leave the boathouse full
   Of citronella and potato salad.

The kodachrome should be a free-hand drawing
   (The bathing beach seen from the bathhouse door)
Showing the sunset on the long withdrawing
   Tide and, dimly, figures on the shore.

JOHN MALCOLM BRINNIN

FROM PAUMANOK STARTING
I FLY LIKE A BIRD

From Paumanok starting I fly like a bird,
Around and around to soar to sing the idea of all,
To the north betaking myself to sing there arctic songs,
To Kanada till I absorb Kanada in myself, to Michigan then,
To Wisconsin, Iowa, Minnesota, to sing their songs,
    (they are inimitable;)
Then to Ohio and Indiana to sing theirs, to Missouri and
    Kansas and Arkansas to sing theirs,
To Tennessee and Kentucky, to the Carolinas and Georgia
    to sing theirs,
To Texas and so along up toward California, to roam
    accepted everywhere;
To sing first, (to the tap of the war-drum if need be,)
The idea of all, of the Western world one and inseparable,
And then the song of each member of these States.

WALT WHITMAN

MANNAHATTA

I was asking for something specific and perfect for my city,
Whereupon lo! upsprang the aboriginal name.

Now I see what there is in a name, a word, liquid, sane,
    unruly, musical, self-sufficient,
I see that the word of my city is that word from of old,
Because I see that word nested in nests of water-bays, superb,
Rich, hemmed thick all around with sail-ships and steam-ships,
    an island sixteen miles long, solid-founded,
Numberless crowded streets, high growths of iron, slender,
    strong, light, splendidly uprising toward clear skies,
Tides swift and ample, well-loved by me, toward sundown,
The flowing sea-currents, the little islands, larger adjoining
    islands, the heights, the villas,
The countless masts, the white shore-steamers, the lighters,
    the ferry-boats, the black sea-steamers well-modelled,
The down-town streets, the jobbers' houses of business, the
    houses of business of the ship-merchants and money-
    brokers, the river-streets,
Immigrants arriving, fifteen or twenty thousand in a week,
The carts hauling goods, the manly race of drivers of horses,
    the brown-faced sailors,
The summer air, the bright sun shining, and the sailing clouds
    aloft,
The winter snows, the sleigh-bells, the broken ice in the river,
    passing along up or down with the flood-tide or ebb-tide,
The mechanics of the city, the masters, well-formed,
    beautiful-faced, looking you straight in the eyes,

Trottoirs thronged, vehicles, Broadway, the women, the
  shops and shows,
A million people—manners free and superb—open voices—
  hospitality—the most courageous and friendly young men,
City of hurried and sparkling waters! city of spires and masts!
City nested in bays! my city!

WALT WHITMAN

THE SPARE QUILT

An art as meagre as a quilt
Of faded colors, oddly matched
From flowers which fading could not wilt
Though to a white like winter's patched.

They pieced, they interlined and stitched,
Since nature would not keep them warm;
And close at night their shoulders twitched
The quilt about them when the storm

Outraged the windows and outside
Shrieked in the uncharitable air.
They knew then that the night was wide
And wished their art had been less spare.

But as the long night settled down,
Shivering from chill to chill,
They felt the darkness like a frown
And felt their work had not been ill.

Hugging the quilt they saw how young
Indulgent hunters shining went
Toward danger, proud, and most when hung
With death, their souls sufficient

To that solitude. It solaced them
That those unshivering sons were stout,
Since they, contented with a dream,
Could only stitch the cold night out.

JOHN PEALE BISHOP

DANIEL BOONE

1735–1820

When Daniel Boone goes by, at night,
The phantom deer arise
And all lost, wild America
Is burning in their eyes.

STEPHEN VINCENT BENÉT

SOUTHERN PINES

White pine, yellow pine,
The first man fearing the forest
Felled trees, afraid of shadow,
His own shade in the shadow of pinewoods.

Slash pine, loblolly,
The second man wore tarheels,
Slashed pine, gashed pine,
The silent land changed to a sea-charge.

Short leaf, long leaf,
The third man had aching pockets.
Mill town, lumber mill,
And buzzards sailed the piney barrens.

Cut pine, burnt pine,
The fourth man's eyes burned in starvation.
Bone-back cattle, razor-back hogs
Achieve the seedling, end the pinewoods.

JOHN PEALE BISHOP

GRANT WOOD'S AMERICAN LANDSCAPE

This is not real: this is the shape of a dream spun
By a strong man with X-ray eyes that see
Through enormous planes of sun the design that no sun
Can reveal clear any more: at best we remember vaguely,
    seeing
These mornings these afternoons these clean
Men and women like a child's long day in the sunlight that
    no one
Remembers any more: it is drenched, it is gone in the sun.

But this is the way it was, and this is the way the old men
Dreamed it in the beginning: proud land with no end:
Patterned with quilt-like honesty and fenced
For honesty but not to keep anyone out or anyone in:
Patterned with the sure line of the plow and the bright line
Of the corn and the colors of soil changing
As far as the sky in the shadows of wind.

                        And this
Is the way it was, but this is not real: these houses white,
Precise, angled with safety, islanded in the rich grass:
These people going and coming at fruitful chores: these barns'
    weight
Solid beyond the fat-cheeked trees in the sun: and the land
    in the sun
Immensely stretched and never too much to roll and reach
Farther than we could say, and everywhere such strictness
Set upon luxury justly: these tracks of the share and the wheel
Show that the men are sure and wise in their labor, they go
    back
And forth too clean and sure: they are not real.

There is too much sun. There is too much peace.

WINFIELD TOWNLEY SCOTT

THE DISTANT RUNNERS

*Six great horses of Spain, set free after his death by De
Soto's men, ran west and restored to America the wild
race lost there some thousands of years ago.*—LEGEND

Ferdinand De Soto lies
Soft again in river mud.
Birds again, as on the day
Of his descending, rise and go
Straightly West, and do not know
Of feet beneath that faintly thud.

If I were there in other time,
Between the proper sky and stream;
If I were there and saw the six
Abandoned manes, and ran along,
I could sing the fetlock song
That now is chilled within a dream.

Ferdinand De Soto, sleeping
In the river, never heard
Four-and-twenty Spanish hooves
Fling off their iron and cut the green,
Leaving circles new and clean
While overhead the wing-tips whirred.

Neither I nor any walker
By the Mississippi now
Can see the dozen nostrils open
Half in pain for death of men;
But half in gladness, neighing then
As loud as loping would allow.

On they rippled, tail and back,
A prairie day, and swallows knew
A dark, uneven current there.
But not a sound came up the wind,
And toward the night their shadow thinned
Before the black that flooded through.

If I were there to bend and look,
The sky would know them as they sped
And turn to see. But I am here,
And they are far, and time is old.
Within my dream the grass is cold;
The legs are locked; the sky is dead.

MARK VAN DOREN

THE RIVER

Stick your patent name on a signboard
brother — all over — going west — young man   . . . and past
Tintex — Japalac — Certain-teed Overalls ads   the din and
and land sakes! under the new playbill ripped   slogans of
                                                  the year—
in the guaranteed corner — see Bert Williams what?
Minstrels when you steal a chicken just
save me the wing for if it isn't
Erie it ain't for miles around a
Mazda — and the telegraphic night coming on Thomas

a Ediford — whistling down the tracks
a headlight rushing with the sound — can you
imagine — while an EXPRESS makes time like
SCIENCE — COMMERCE and the HOLYGHOST
RADIO ROARS IN EVERY HOME WE HAVE THE NORTHPOLE
WALLSTREET AND VIRGINBIRTH WITHOUT STONES OR
WIRES OR EVEN RUNning brooks connecting ears
and no more sermons windows flashing roar
Breathtaking — as you like it . . . eh?

So the 20th Century — so
whizzed the Limited — roared by and left
three men, still hungry on the tracks, ploddingly
watching the tail lights wizen and converge, slip-
ping gimleted and neatly out of sight.
*

The last bear, shot drinking in the Dakotas
Loped under wires that span the mountain stream.
Keen instruments, strung to a vast precision
Bind town to town and dream to ticking dream.

But some men take their liquor slow — and count
— Though they'll confess no rosary nor clue —
The river's minute by the far brook's year.
Under a world of whistles, wires and steam
Caboose-like they go ruminating through
Ohio, Indiana — blind baggage —
To Cheyenne tagging . . . Maybe Kalamazoo.

Time's rendings, time's blendings they construe
As final reckonings of fire and snow;
Strange bird-wit, like the elemental gist
Of unwalled winds they offer, singing low
My Old Kentucky Home and *Casey Jones*,
Some Sunny Day. I heard a road-gang chanting so.
And afterwards, who had a colt's eyes — one said,
"Jesus! Oh I remember watermelon days!" And sped
High in a cloud of merriment, recalled
"— And when my Aunt Sally Simpson smiled," he drawled —
"It was almost Louisiana, long ago."

"There's no place like Booneville though, Buddy,"
One said, excising a last burr from his vest,
"— For early trouting." Then peering in the can,
"— But I kept on the tracks." Possessed, resigned,
He trod the fire down pensively and grinned,
Spreading dry shingles of a beard. . . .

Behind

My father's cannery works I used to see
Rail-squatters ranged in nomad raillery,
The ancient men — wifeless or runaway
Hobo-trekkers that forever search
An empire wilderness of freight and rails.
Each seemed a child, like me, on a loose perch,
Holding to childhood like some termless play.
John, Jake or Charley, hopping the slow freight
— Memphis to Tallahassee — riding the rods,
Blind fists of nothing, humpty-dumpty clods.

Yet they touch something like a key perhaps.
From pole to pole across the hills, the states
— They know a body under the wide rain;
Youngsters with eyes like fjords, old reprobates
With racetrack jargon,—dotting immensity
They lurk across her, knowing her yonder breast
Snow-silvered, sumac-stained or smoky blue —
Is past the valley-sleepers, south or west.
— As I have trod the rumorous midnights, too,

but who have
touched her,
knowing her
without name

And past the circuit of the lamp's thin flame
(O Nights that brought me to her body bare!)
Have dreamed beyond the print that bound her name.
Trains sounding the long blizzards out — I heard
Wail into distances I knew were hers.
Papooses crying on the wind's long mane
Screamed redskin dynastic that fled the brain,
— Dead echoes! But I knew her body there,
Time like a serpent down her shoulder, dark,
And space, an eaglet's wing, laid on her hair.

Under the Ozarks, domed by Iron Mountain,
The old gods of the rain lie wrapped in pools
Where eyeless fish curvet a sunken fountain   nor the
And re-descend with corn from querulous crows.   myths of her
Such pilferings make up their timeless eatage,   fathers . . .
Propitiate them for their timber torn
By iron, iron — always the iron dealt cleavage!
They doze now, below axe and powder horn.

And Pullman breakfasters glide glistening steel
From tunnel into field — iron strides the dew —
Straddles the hill, a dance of wheel on wheel.
You have a half-hour's wait at Siskiyou,
Or stay the night and take the next train through.
Southward, near Cairo passing, you can see
The Ohio merging, — borne down Tennessee;
And if it's summer and the sun's in dusk
Maybe the breeze will lift the River's musk
— As though the waters breathed that you might know
Memphis Johnny, Steamboat Bill, Missouri Joe.
Oh, lean from the window, if the train slows down,
As though you touched hands with some ancient clown,
— A little while gaze absently below
And hum *Deep River* with them while they go.

Yes, turn again and sniff once more — look see,
O Sheriff, Brakeman and Authority —
Hitch up your pants and crunch another quid,
For you, too, feed the River timelessly.
And few evade full measure of their fate;
Always they smile out eerily what they seem.
I could believe he joked at heaven's gate —
Dan Midland — jolted from the cold brake-beam.

Down, down — born pioneers in time's despite,
Grimed tributaries to an ancient flow —
They win no frontier by their wayward plight,
But drift in stillness, as from Jordan's brow.

You will not hear it as the sea; even stone
Is not more hushed by gravity . . . But slow,
As loth to take more tribute — sliding prone
Like one whose eyes were buried long ago

The River, spreading, flows — and spends your dream.
What are you, lost within this tideless spell?
You are your father's father, and the stream —
A liquid theme that floating niggers swell.

Damp tonnage and alluvial march of days —
Nights turbid, vascular with silted shale
And roots surrendered down of moraine clays:
The Mississippi drinks the farthest dale.

O quarrying passion, undertowed sunlight!
The basalt surface drags a jungle grace
Ochreous and lynx-barred in lengthening might;
Patience! and you shall reach the biding place!

Over De Soto's bones the freighted floors
Throb past the City storied of three thrones.
Down two more turns the Mississippi pours
(Anon tall ironsides up from salt lagoons)

And flows within itself, heaps itself free.
All fades but one thin skyline 'round . . . Ahead
No embrace opens but the stinging sea;
The River lifts itself from its long bed,

Poised wholly on its dream, a mustard glow
Tortured with history, its one will — flow!
— The Passion spreads in wide tongues, choked and slow,
Meeting the Gulf, hosannas silently below.

HART CRANE

MINNESOTA THANKSGIVING

For that free Grace bringing us past terrible risks
& thro' great griefs surviving to this feast
sober & still, with the children unborn and born,
among brave friends, Lord, we stand again in debt
and find ourselves in the glad position: Gratitude.

We praise our ancestors who delivered us here
within warm walls all safe, aware of music,
likely toward ample & attractive meat
with whatever accompaniment
Kate in her kind ingenuity has seen fit to devise,

and we hope — across the most strange year to come —
continually to do them and You not sufficient honour
but such as we become able to devise
out of a decent or joyful *conscience* & thanksgiving.
Yippee!
      Bless then, as Thou wilt, this wilderness board.

JOHN BERRYMAN

THE CLOSING OF THE RODEO

The lariat snaps; the cowboy rolls
  His pack, and mounts and rides away.
Back to the land the cowboy goes.

Plumes of smoke from the factory sway
  In the setting sun. The curtain falls,
A train in the darkness pulls away.

Good-by, says the rain on the iron roofs.
  Good-by, say the barber poles.
Dark drum the vanishing horses' hooves.

WILLIAM JAY SMITH

THE TESTAMENT
OF PERPETUAL CHANGE

Mortal Prudence, handmaid of divine Providence
    Walgreen carries Culture to the West:
hath inscrutable reckoning with Fate and Fortune:
    At Cortez, Colorado the Indian prices
We sail a changeful sea through halcyon days and storm,
    a bottle of cheap perfume, furtively —
and when the ship laboreth, our stedfast purpose
    but doesn't buy, while under my hotel window
trembles like as a compass in a binnacle.
    a Radiance Rose spreads its shell — thin
Our stability is but balance, and wisdom lies
    petals above the non-irrigated garden
in masterful administration of the unforeseen
    among the unprotected desert foliage.

'Twas late in my long journey when I had clomb to where
    Having returned from Mesa Verde, the ruins
the path was narrowing and the company few
    of the Cliff Dwellers' palaces still in possession of my mind.

WILLIAM CARLOS WILLIAMS

THE SAND PAINTERS
(*New Mexico*)

The thumb, for a summer's promise,
Leans to its shadow on the cloud-colored sand
And measures its wilderness crystal to a line . . .

The shadow deploys, and the cloud, and the catch of the
    singer,
Leaving the pure stroke after the considering hand,
Wise in an animal stealth, abstemious, fine:

    The small-headed goddess . . . fasces of hemlock and
       arrows . . .
    Miraculous sunwheel, bound in a bowcord strain . . .
    The side-pointing buffalo eyes in a pumice of mirrors . . .

Returns. Recoils. The enormous web moves under.
The cloud sways westward, poising a pyramid stain.
The Spinner ascends the loom of meridian,
While, through the sift of his finger,
A thong in the hourglass trembles from thunder to thunder
And empties a season of rain.

BEN BELITT

BY FRAZIER CREEK FALLS

Standing up on lifted, folded rock
looking out and down —

The creek falls to a far valley.
hills beyond that
facing, half-forested, dry
— clear sky
strong wind in the
stiff glittering needle clusters
of the pine — their brown
round trunk bodies
straight, still;
rustling trembling limbs and twigs

listen.

This living flowing land
is all there is, forever

We *are* it
it sings through us —

We could live on this Earth
without clothes or tools!

GARY SNYDER

THE TRAIL BESIDE
THE RIVER PLATTE

He saw, abandoned to the sand,
"claw-footed tables, once well waxed
and rubbed, or massive bureaus
of carved oak," now blistered,

sun-scorched, and warped.
So, the Ogillallah lived
as they had lived, rode
their ponies where the plains

were still humped black with buffalo —
enough, it seemed,
for the whole country
to feast on tongues, forever.

But the herds, of course, were doomed,
and the "large wandering communities"
that followed them would follow them
to nowhere. Parkman remembered

a day when innumerable animals thundered
into a ravine:
"Hoofs were jerked upwards," he said,
"tails flourished

in the air, and amid a cloud
of dust, the buffalo seemed
to sink into the earth
before me."

WILLIAM HEYEN

Francis Parkman (1823-1893) was an American historian who in 1846 fol-
lowed the pioneer trail from St. Louis to Oregon. John Fiske described him
as the "first great writer who . . . understood the Indian's character and
motives."—H.P.

THE CALIFORNIA OAKS

Spreading and low, unwatered, concentrate
Of years of growth that thickens, not expands,
With leaves like mica and with roots that grate
Upon the deep foundations of these lands,
In your brown shadow, on your heavy loam
— Leaves shrinking to the whisper of decay —
What feet have come to roam,
                              what eyes to stay?
Your motion has o'ertaken what calm hands?

Quick as a sunbeam, when a bird divides
The lesser branches, on impassive ground,
Hwui-Shan,* the ancient, for a moment glides,
Demure with wisdom, and without a sound;
Brown feet that come to meet him, quick and shy,
Move in the flesh, then, browner, dry to bone;
The brook-like shadows lie
                              where sun had shone;
Ceaseless, the dead leaves gather, mound on mound.

And where they gather, darkening the glade,
In hose and doublet, and with knotty beard,
Armed with the musket and the pirate's blade,
Stern as the silence by the savage feared,
Drake and his seamen pause to view the hills,

---

*There is a brief account of Hwui-Shan on pages 24-5 of *A History of California; the Spanish Period*, by Charles Edward Chapman. Hwui-Shan was a Chinese Buddhist priest, who may have come to California in 499 A.D. According to Chapman, the story is found in Volume 231 of the great Chinese Encyclopedia and is found in other works and has long been known to Chinese scholars. Chapman believes that there were other Chinese voyages to the west coast of North America at very early dates.—Y.W.

Measure the future with a steady gaze.
But when they go naught fills
                        the patient days;
The bay lies empty where the vessels cleared.

The Spaniard, learning caution from the trees,
Building his dwelling from the native clay,
Took native concubines: the blood of these
Calming his blood, he made a longer stay.
Longer, but yet recessive, for the change
Came on his sons and their sons to the end;
For peace may yet derange
                        and earth may bend
The ambitious mind to an archaic way.

Then the invasion! and the soil was turned,
The hidden waters drained, the valleys dried;
And whether fire or purer sunlight burned,
No matter! one by one the old oaks died.
Died or are dying! The archaic race —
Black oak, live oak, and valley oak — ere long
Must crumble on the place
                        which they made strong
And in the calm they guarded now abide.

YVOR WINTERS

AMERICAN NAMES

I have fallen in love with American names,
The sharp names that never get fat,
The snakeskin-titles of mining-claims,
The plumed war-bonnet of Medicine Hat,
Tucson and Deadwood and Lost Mule Flat.

Seine and Piave are silver spoons,
But the spoonbowl-metal is thin and worn,
There are English counties like hunting-tunes
Played on the keys of a postboy's horn,
But I will remember where I was born.

I will remember Carquinez Straits,
Little French Lick and Lundy's Lane,
The Yankee ships and the Yankee dates
And the bullet-towns of Calamity Jane.
I will remember Skunktown Plain.

I will fall in love with a Salem tree
And a rawhide quirt from Santa Cruz,
I will get me a bottle of Boston sea
And a blue-gum nigger to sing me blues.
I am tired of loving a foreign muse.

Rue des Martyrs and Bleeding-Heart-Yard,
Senlis, Pisa, and Blindman's Oast,
It is a magic ghost you guard
But I am sick for a newer ghost,
Harrisburg, Spartanburg, Painted Post.

Henry and John were never so
And Henry and John were always right?
Granted, but when it was time to go
And the tea and the laurels had stood all night,
Did they never watch for Nantucket Light?

I shall not rest quiet in Montparnasse.
I shall not lie easy at Winchelsea.
You may bury my body in Sussex grass,
You may bury my tongue at Champmédy.
I shall not be there. I shall rise and pass.
Bury my heart at Wounded Knee.

STEPHEN VINCENT BENÉT

The stepping stones to thee
to-day and here, America

✵ ✵ *HISTORY*

FEBRUARY 22

Three boys, American, in dungarees,
walk at a slant across the street
against the mild slant of the winter sun,
moseying out this small, still holiday.

The back of the cold is broken; later snows
will follow, mixed with rain, but today
the macadam is bare, the sun loops high,
and the trees are bathed in sweet grayness.

He was a perfect hero: a man of stone,
as colorless as a monument,
anonymous as Shakespeare. We know him
only as the author of his deeds.

There may have been a man: a surveyor,
a wencher, a temper, a stubborn farmer's mind;
but our legends seem impertinent
gaieties scratched upon his granite.

He gazes at us from our dollar bills
reproachfully, a strange green lady,
heavy-lidded, niggle-lipped, and wigged,
who served us better than we have deserved.

More than great successes, we love great failures.
Lincoln is Messiah; he, merely Caesar.
He suffered greatness like a curse.
He fathered our country, we feel, without great joy.

But let us love him now, for he crossed the famous ice,
brought us out of winter, stood, and surveyed
the breadth of our land exulting in the sun:
looked forward to the summer that is past.

JOHN UPDIKE

107

ON A FORTIFICATION AT BOSTON BEGUN BY WOMEN

*Dux Foemina Facti**

A Grand attempt some Amazonian Dames
Contrive whereby to glorify their names,
A Ruff for *Boston* Neck of mud and turfe,
Reaching from side to side from surfe to surfe,
Their nimble hands spin up like Christmas pyes,
Their pastry by degrees on high doth rise.
The wheel at home counts it an holiday,
Since while the Mistris worketh it may play.
A tribe of female hands, but manly hearts
Forsake at home their pasty-crust and tarts
To knead the dirt, the samplers down they hurle,
Their undulating silks they closely furle.
The pick-axe one as a Commandress holds,
While t'other at her awkness gently scolds.

---

*Virgil, *Aeneid* I. 364: The leader is a woman. A motto used on medals struck in 1588 after Elizabeth I's victory over the Spanish Armada.

Though Tompson's meter is somewhat unpolished, even crude in places, he has a lively, hard-driving pace and a perceptive eye for situations. For example, in his mock-epic portrait of the ludicrous attempt by a group of women to defend Boston against the Indians with a "Ruff" of "mud and turfe" he combines a gently satiric chuckle at their ineffectualness with admiration for the spirit of the endeavor. It is his ability to take a whole view of situations and events, and to fix them with graphic completeness, that makes Tompson an important poet of early America.

And he is a particularly American poet, the first to publish in America a volume of poetry about the country. He may sprinkle classical references throughout his work, but Tompson's eye is steadily on the land and its inhabitants. His Indians are American ones, not European conceptions of Indians.—Harrison T. Meserole, *Seventeenth-Century American Poetry*

This poem was published during King Philip's War (1675–76), a war against border settlements in New England led by King Philip, sachem of the Wampanoag tribe.—H.P.

One puffs and sweats, the other mutters why
Cant you promove your work so fast as I?
Some dig, some delve, and others hands do feel
The little waggons weight with single wheel.
And least some fainting fits the weak surprize,
They want no sack nor cakes, they are more wise.
These brave essayes draw forth Male stronger hands
More like to Dawbers than to Martial bands:
These do the work, and sturdy bulwarks raise,
But the beginners well deserve the praise.

BENJAMIN TOMPSON

from McFINGAL

Rise then, ere ruin swift surprize,
To victory, to vengeance rise!
Hark, how the distant din alarms!
The echoing trumpet breathes, to arms:
From provinces remote, afar,
The sons of glory rouze to war;
'Tis freedom calls; th' enraptur'd sound
The Apalachian hills rebound;
The Georgian shores her voice shall hear,
And start from lethargies of fear.
From the parch'd zone, with glowing ray,
Where pours the sun intenser day,
To shores where icy waters roll,
And tremble to the dusky pole,
Inspir'd by freedom's heav'nly charms,
United nations wake to arms.
The star of conquest lights their way,
And guides their vengeance on their prey—
Yes, tho' tyrannic force oppose,
Still shall they triumph o'er their foes,
Till heav'n the happy land shall bless,
With safety, liberty and peace.

JOHN TRUMBULL

STANZAS

On the Decease of Thomas Paine,
Who Died at New York,
on the 8th of June, 1809

Princes and kings decay and die
  And, instant, rise again:
But this is not the case, trust me,
  With men like THOMAS PAINE.

In vain the democratic host
  His *equal* would attain:
For years to come they will not boast
  A second Thomas Paine.

Though many may his name assume;
  Assumption is in vain;
For every man has not his plume—
  Whose name is *Thomas Paine.*

Though heaven bestow'd on all its sons
  Their *proper* share of brain,
It gives to few, ye simple ones,
  The mind of Thomas Paine.

To tyrants and the tyrant crew,
  Indeed, he was the bane;
He writ, and gave them all their due,
  And signed it,—THOMAS PAINE.

Oh! how we loved to see him write
   And curb the race of Cain!
They hope and wish that Thomas P——
   May never rise again.

What idle hopes!—yes—such a man
   May yet appear again,—
When *they* are dead they die for aye:
   —Not so with Thomas Paine.

PHILIP FRENEAU

WARREN'S ADDRESS AT BUNKER HILL

[June 16–17, 1775]

Stand! the ground's your own, my braves!
Will ye give it up to slaves?
Will ye look for greener graves?

Hope ye mercy still?
What's the mercy despots feel?
Hear it in that battle-peal!
Read it on yon bristling steel!
Ask it,—ye who will.

Fear ye foes who kill for hire?
Will ye to your homes retire?
Look behind you!—they're afire!
And, before you, see
Who have done it! From the vale
On they come—and will ye quail?
Leaden rain and iron hail
Let their welcome be!

In the God of battles trust!
Die we may,—and die we must:
But, O, where can dust to dust
Be consigned so well,
As where heaven its dews shall shed
On the martyred patriot's bed,
And the rocks shall raise their head,
Of his deeds to tell?

JOHN PIERPONT

from UNDER THE OLD ELM

Poem read at Cambridge on the hundredth anniversary
of Washington's taking command of the American Army,
3d July, 1775

1.

Never to see a nation born
Hath been given to mortal man,
Unless to those who, on that summer morn,
Gazed silent when the great Virginian
Unsheathed the sword whose fatal flash
Shot union through the incoherent clash
Of our loose atoms, crystallizing them
Around a single will's unpliant stem,
And making purpose of emotion rash.
Out of that scabbard sprang, as from its womb,
Nebulous at first but hardening to a star,
Through mutual share of sunburst and of gloom,
The common faith that made us what we are.

2.

That lifted blade transformed our jangling clans,
Till then provincial, to Americans,
And made a unity of wildering plans;
Here was the doom fixed: here is marked the date
When this New World awoke to man's estate.
Burnt its last ship and ceased to look behind:
Nor thoughtless was the choice; no love or hate
Could from its poise that deliberate mind,
Weighing between too early and too late
Those pitfalls of the man refused by Fate:
His was the impartial vision of the great
Who see not as they wish, but as they find.

He saw the dangers of defeat, nor less
The incomputable perils of success;
The sacred past thrown by, an empty rind;
The future, cloud-land, snare of prophets blind;
The waste of war, the ignominy of peace;
On either hand a sullen rear of woes,
Whose garnered lightnings none could guess,
Piling its thunder-heads and muttering "Cease!"
Yet drew not back his hand, but gravely chose
The seeming-desperate task whence our new nation rose.

JAMES RUSSELL LOWELL

THE WALLABOUT MARTYRS

(In Brooklyn, in an old vault, mark'd by no special recognition, lie huddled at this moment the undoubtedly authentic remains of the stanchest and earliest Revolutionary patriots from the British prison ships and prisons of the times of 1776-83, in and around New York, and from all over Long Island; originally buried—many thousands of them —in trenches in the Wallabout sands.)

Greater than memory of Achilles or Ulysses,
More, more by far to thee than tomb of Alexander,
Those cart loads of old charnel ashes, scales and splints of
    mouldy bones,
Once living men—once resolute courage, aspiration, strength,
The stepping stones to thee to-day and here, America.

WALT WHITMAN

CONCORD HYMN

Sung at the Completion of the Battle Monument,
April 19, 1836

By the rude bridge that arched the flood,
    Their flag to April's breeze unfurled,
Here once the embattled farmers stood,
    And fired the shot heard round the world.

The foe long since in silence slept;
    Alike the conqueror silent sleeps;
And Time the ruined bridge has swept
    Down the dark stream which seaward creeps.

On this green bank, by this soft stream,
    We set to-day a votive stone;
That memory may their deed redeem,
    When, like our sires, our sons are gone.

Spirit, that made those heroes dare
    To die, and leave their children free,
Bid Time and Nature gently spare
    The shaft we raise to them and thee.

RALPH WALDO EMERSON

My country need not change her gown,
Her triple suit as sweet
As when 'twas cut at Lexington,
And first pronounced "a fit."

Great Britain disapproves, "the stars";
Disparagement discreet,—
There's something in their attitude
That taunts her bayonet.

EMILY DICKINSON

OLD IRONSIDES

[September 14, 1830]

Ay, tear her tattered ensign down!
　　Long has it waved on high,
And many an eye has danced to see
　　That banner in the sky,
Beneath it rung the battle shout,
　　And burst the cannon's roar;—
The meteor of the ocean air
　　Shall sweep the clouds no more.

Her deck, once red with heroes' blood,
　　Where dwelt the vanquished foe,
When winds were hurrying o'er the flood,
　　And waves were white below,
No more shall feel the victor's tread,
　　Or know the conquered knee;—
The harpies of the shore shall pluck
　　The eagle of the sea!

Oh, better that her shattered hulk
　　Should sink beneath the wave;
Her thunders shook the mighty deep,
　　And there should be her grave;
Nail to the mast her holy flag,
　　Set every threadbare sail,
And give her to the god of storms,
　　The lightning and the gale!

OLIVER WENDELL HOLMES

"Old Ironsides" is the nickname of the *Constitution,* the frigate which won
the first American naval victory in the War of 1812. This poem effectively
stirred up public opinion when the Navy ordered the demolition of the
historic vessel, now moored in Boston.—H.P.

ABRAHAM LINCOLN
WALKS AT MIDNIGHT

(In Springfield, Illinois)

It is portentous, and a thing of state
That here at midnight, in our little town
A mourning figure walks, and will not rest,
Near the old court-house pacing up and down,

Or by his homestead, or in shadowed yards
He lingers where his children used to play,
Or through the market, on the well-worn stones
He stalks until the dawn-stars burn away.

A bronzed, lank man! His suit of ancient black,
A famous high top-hat and plain worn shawl
Make him the quaint great figure that men love,
The prairie-lawyer, master of us all.

He cannot sleep upon his hillside now.
He is among us:—as in times before!
And we who toss and lie awake for long
Breathe deep, and start, to see him pass the door.

His head is bowed. He thinks on men and kings.
Yea, when the sick world cries, how can he sleep?
Too many peasants fight, they know not why,
Too many homesteads in black terror weep.

The sins of all the war-lords burn his heart.
He sees the dreadnaughts scouring every main.
He carries on his shawl-wrapped shoulders now
The bitterness, the folly and the pain.

He cannot rest until a spirit-dawn
Shall come;—the shining hope of Europe free:
The league of sober folk, the Workers' Earth,
Bringing long peace to Cornland, Alp and Sea.

It breaks his heart that kings must murder still,
That all his hours of travail here for men
Seem yet in vain. And who will bring white peace
That he may sleep upon his hill again?

VACHEL LINDSAY

FREDERICK DOUGLASS

When it is finally ours, this freedom, this liberty, this beautiful
and terrible thing, needful to man as air,
usable as earth; when it belongs at last to all,
when it is truly instinct, brain matter, diastole, systole,
reflex action; when it is finally won; when it is more
than the gaudy mumbo jumbo of politicians:
this man, this Douglass, this former slave, this Negro
beaten to his knees, exiled, visioning a world
where none is lonely, none hunted, alien,
this man, superb in love and logic, this man
shall be remembered. Oh, not with statues' rhetoric,
not with legends and poems and wreaths of bronze alone,
but with the lives grown out of his life, the lives
fleshing his dream of the beautiful, needful thing.

ROBERT E. HAYDEN

Frederick Douglass (1817–1895) was an escaped slave who bought his free-
dom in 1847. He founded a newspaper called *Northern Star* and was active
in the antislavery movement. He was also a firm supporter of women's
suffrage.—H.P.

THE WITNESSES

In Ocean's wide domains,
    Half buried in the sands,
Lie skeletons in chains,
    With shackled feet and hands.

Beyond the fall of dews,
    Deeper than plummet lies,
Float ships, with all their crews,
    No more to sink nor rise.

There the black Slave-ship swims,
    Freighted with human forms,
Whose fettered, fleshless limbs
    Are not the sport of storms.

These are the bones of Slaves;
    They gleam from the abyss;
They cry, from yawning waves,
    "We are the Witnesses!"

Within Earth's wide domains
    Are markets for men's lives;
Their necks are galled with chains,
    Their wrists are cramped with gyves.

Dead bodies, that the kite
    In deserts makes its prey;
Murders, that with affright
    Scare school-boys from their play!

All evil thoughts and deeds;
   Anger, and lust, and pride;
The foulest, rankest weeds,
   That choke Life's groaning tide!

These are the woes of Slaves;
   They glare from the abyss;
They cry, from unknown graves,
   "We are the Witnesses!"

HENRY WADSWORTH LONGFELLOW

Why did all manly gifts in Webster fail?
He wrote on Nature's grandest brow, *For Sale*

RALPH WALDO EMERSON

Daniel Webster, more intent on saving the Union than on freeing the slaves, supported the Compromise of 1850. Emerson was deeply disillusioned by this move: he refused to obey the Fugitive Slave Law and took a firm stand against slavery.—H.P.

THE SLAVE SINGING
AT MIDNIGHT

Loud he sang the psalm of David!
He, a Negro and enslavèd,
Sang of Israel's victory,
Sang of Zion, bright and free.

In that hour, when night is calmest,
Sang he from the Hebrew Psalmist,
In a voice so sweet and clear
That I could not choose but hear,

Songs of triumph, and ascriptions,
Such as reached the swart Egyptians,
When upon the Red Sea coast
Perished Pharaoh and his host.

And the voice of his devotion
Filled my soul with strange emotion;
For its tones by turns were glad,
Sweetly solemn, wildly sad.

Paul and Silas, in their prison,
Sang of Christ, the Lord arisen.
And an earthquake's arm of might
Broke their dungeon-gates at night.

But, alas! what holy angel
Brings the Slave this glad evangel?
And what earthquake's arm of might
Breaks his dungeon-gates at night?

                    HENRY WADSWORTH LONGFELLOW

FROM TROLLOPE'S JOURNAL

Winter, 1861

As far as statues go, so far there's not
much choice: they're either Washingtons
or Indians, a whitewashed, stubby lot,
His country's Father or His foster sons.
The White House in a sad, unhealthy spot
just higher than Potomac's swampy brim,
— they say the present President has got
ague or fever in each backwoods limb.
On Sunday afternoon I wandered, — rather,
I floundered, — out alone. The air was raw
and dark; the marsh half-ice, half-mud. This weather
is normal now: a frost, and then a thaw,
and then a frost. A hunting man, I found
the Pennsylvania Avenue heavy ground...
There all around me in the ugly mud,
— hoof-pocked, uncultivated, — herds of cattle,
numberless, wond'ring steers and oxen, stood:
beef for the Army, after the next battle.
Their legs were caked the color of dried blood;
their horns were wreathed with fog. Poor, starving, dumb
or lowing creatures, never to chew the cud
or fill their maws again! Th'effluvium
made that damned anthrax on my forehead throb.
I called a surgeon in, a young man, but,
with a sore throat himself, he did his job.
We talked about the War, and as he cut
away, he croaked out, "Sir, I do declare
everyone's sick! The soldiers poison the air."

ELIZABETH BISHOP

LITTLE GIFFEN

Out of the focal and foremost fire,
Out of the hospital walls as dire,
Smitten of grape-shot and gangrene
(Eighteenth battle and *he* sixteen!) —
Spectre such as you seldom see,
Little Giffen of Tennessee.

"Take him and welcome!" the surgeon said;
"Little the doctor can help the dead!"
So we took him and brought him where
The balm was sweet on the summer air;
And we laid him down on a wholesome bed —
Utter Lazarus, heel to head!

And we watched the war with bated breath —
Skeleton Boy against skeleton Death.
Months of torture, how many such!
Weary weeks of the stick and crutch;
And still a glint in the steel-blue eye
Told of a spirit that wouldn't die, —

And didn't. Nay, more! in death's despite
The crippled skeleton learned to write.
"Dear Mother," at first, of course; and then,
"Dear Captain," inquiring about "the men."
Captain's answer: "Of eighty-and-five,
Giffen and I are left alive."

Word of gloom from the war, one day:
"Johnston's pressed at the front, they say!"*
Little Giffen was up and away;
A tear — his first — as he bade good-by,
Dimmed the glint of his steel-blue eye.
"I'll write, if spared." There was news of the fight;
But none of Giffen. — He did not write.

I sometimes fancy that, were I king
Of the princely Knights of the Golden Ring,
With the song of the minstrel in mine ear,
And the tender legend that trembles here,
I'd give the best on his bended knee,
The whitest soul of my chivalry,
For Little Giffen of Tennessee.

FRANCIS ORRAY TICKNOR

*Joseph E. Johnston was a general in the Confederate Army.—H.P.

ODE

*Sung on the occasion of decorating the graves
of the Confederate dead, at Magnolia Cemetery,
Charleston, S.C., 1867*

Sleep sweetly in your humble graves,
    Sleep, martyrs of a fallen cause;
Though yet no marble column craves
    The pilgrim here to pause.

In seeds of laurel in the earth
    The blossom of your fame is blown,
And somewhere, waiting for its birth,
    The shaft is in the stone!

Meanwhile, behalf the tardy years
    Which keep in trust your storied tombs,
Behold! your sisters bring their tears,
    And these memorial blooms.

Small tributes! but your shades will smile
    More proudly on these wreaths to-day,
Than when some cannon-moulded pile
    Shall overlook this bay.

Stoop, angels, hither from the skies!
    There is no holier spot of ground
Than where defeated valor lies,
    By mourning beauty crowned!

HENRY TIMROD

A MEDITATION

How often in the years that close,
   When truce had stilled the sieging gun,
The soldiers, mounting on their works,
   With mutual curious glance have run
From face to face along the fronting show,
And kinsman spied, or friend — even in a foe.

What thoughts conflicting than were shared,
   While sacred tenderness perforce
Welled from the heart and wet the eye;
   And something of a strange remorse
Rebelled against the sanctioned sin of blood,
And Christian wars of natural brotherhood.

Then stirred the god within the breast —
   The witness that is man's at birth;
A deep misgiving undermined
   Each plea and subterfuge of earth;
They felt in that rapt pause, with warning rife,
Horror and anguish for the civil strife.

Of North or South they recked not then,
   Warm passion cursed the cause of war:
Can Africa pay back this blood
   Spilt on Potomac's shore?
Yet doubts, as pangs, were vain the strife to stay,
And hands that fain had clasped again could slay.

How frequent in the camp was seen
   The herald from the hostile one,
A guest and frank companion there
   When the proud formal talk was done;
The pipe of peace was smoked even 'mid the war,
And fields in Mexico again fought o'er.
In Western battle long they lay
   So near opposed in trench or pit,
That foeman unto foeman called
   As men who screened in tavern sit:
"You bravely fight" each to the other said —
"Toss us a biscuit!" o'er the wall it sped.

And pale on those same slopes, a boy —
   A stormer, bled in noon-day glare;
No aid the Blue-coats then could bring,
   He cried to them who nearest were,
And out there came 'mid howling shot and shell
A daring foe who him befriended well.

Mark the great Captains on both sides,
   The soldiers with the broad renown —
They all were messmates on the Hudson's marge,
   Beneath one roof they laid them down;
And, free from hate in many an after pass,
Strove as in school-boy rivalry of the class.

A darker side there is; but doubt
   In Nature's charity hovers there:
If men for new agreement`yearn,
   Then old upbraiding best forbear:
"*The South's the sinner!*" Well, so let it be;
But shall the North sin worse, and stand the Pharisee?

O, now that brave men yield the sword,
   Mine be the manful soldier-view;
By how much more they boldly warred,
   By so much more is mercy due:
When Vicksburg fell, and the moody files marched out,
Silent the victors stood, scorning to raise a shout.

HERMAN MELVILLE

133

"O CAPTAIN! MY CAPTAIN!"

[Abraham Lincoln, 1809-1865]

O Captain! my Captain! our fearful trip is done,
The ship has weathered every rack, the prize we sought is won,
The port is near, the bells I hear, the people all exulting,
While follow eyes the steady keel, the vessel grim and daring
    But O heart! heart! heart!
      O the bleeding drops of red,
    Where on the deck my Captain lies,
      Fallen cold and dead.

O Captain! my Captain! rise up and hear the bells;
Rise up — for you the flag is flung — for you the bugle trills,
For you bouquets and ribboned wreaths — for you the shores
  a-crowding,
For you they call, the swaying mass, their eager faces turning;
    Here Captain! dear father!
      This arm beneath your head!
    It is some dream that on the deck
      You've fallen cold and dead.

My Captain does not answer, his lips are pale and still,
My father does not feel my arm, he has no pulse nor will,
The ship is anchored safe and sound, its voyage closed and done,
From fearful trip the victor ship comes in with object won;
    Exult O shores, and ring O bells!
      But I with mournful tread,
    Walk the deck my Captain lies,
      Fallen cold and dead.

WALT WHITMAN

HISTORY AMONG THE ROCKS

There are many ways to die
Here among the rocks in any weather:
Wind, down the eastern gap, will lie
Level along the snow, beating the cedar,
And lull the drowsy head that it blows over
To startle a cold and crystalline dream forever.

The hound's black paw will print the grass in May,
And sycamores rise down a dark ravine,
Where a creek in flood, sucking the rock and clay,
Will tumble the laurel, the sycamore away.
Think how a body, naked and lean
And white as the splintered sycamore, would go
Tumbling and turning, hushed in the end,
With hair afloat in waters that gently bend
To ocean where the blind tides flow.

Under the shadow of ripe wheat,
By flat limestone, will coil the copperhead,
Fanged as the sunlight, hearing the reaper's feet.
But there are other ways, the lean men said:
In these autumn orchards once young men lay dead —
Gray coats, blue coats. Young men on the mountainside
Clambered, fought. Heels muddied the rocky spring.
Their reason is hard to guess, remembering
Blood on their black mustaches in moonlight.
Their reason is hard to guess and a long time past:
The apple falls, falling in the quiet night.

ROBERT PENN WARREN

HUNTING CIVIL WAR RELICS
AT NIMBLEWILL CREEK

As he moves the mine detector
A few inches over the ground,
Making it vitally float
Among the ferns and weeds,
I come into this war
Slowly, with my one brother,
Watching his face grow deep
Between the earphones,
For I can tell
If we enter the buried battle
Of Nimblewill
Only by his expression.

Softly he wanders, parting
The grass with a dreaming hand.
No dead cry yet takes root
In his clapped ears
Or can be seen in his smile.
But underfoot I feel
The dead regroup,
The burst metals all in place,
The battle lines be drawn
Anew to include us
In Nimblewill,
And I carry the shovel and pick

More as if they were
Bright weapons that I bore.
A bird's cry breaks
In two, and into three parts.
We cross the creek; the cry
Shifts into another,
Nearer, bird, and is
Like the shout of a shadow —
Lived-with, appallingly close —
Or the soul, pronouncing
"Nimblewill":
Three tones; your being changes.

We climb the bank;
A faint light glows
On my brother's mouth.
I listen, as two birds fight
For a single voice, but he
Must be hearing the grave,
In pieces, all singing
To his clamped head,
For he smiles as if
He rose from the dead within
Green Nimblewill
And stood in his grandson's shape.

No shot from the buried war
Shall kill me now,
For the dead have waited here
A hundred years to create
Only the look on the face
Of my one brother,
Who stands among them, offering
A metal dish
Afloat in the trembling weeds,
With a long-buried light on his lips
At Nimblewill
And the dead outsinging two birds.

I choke the handle
Of the pick; and fall to my knees
To dig wherever he points,
To bring up mess tin or bullet,
To go underground
Still singing, myself,
Without a sound,
Like a man who renounces war,
Or one who shall lift up the past,
Not breathing "Father,"
At Nimblewill,
But saying, "Fathers! Fathers!"

JAMES DICKEY

THE PLAQUE
IN THE READING ROOM
FOR MY CLASSMATES
KILLED IN KOREA

The sky is a dead fish.
Magnolia petals in mid-May rain
fall like scales off its white belly.
They stick on the fishwife hands
of the library. Wisteria vines are the veins
of childhood wrapping the thighs with wishes,
rising high in the throat to the golden dome
where the evening bell swings. *Finis.*
Down come the loneliest, home.
Schoolboys crouch in the light blue rooms
of the hollow belly, turning the States
over and over, page by page.
The sky keeps falling; gentle doom.

A baseball boy with big eyes unfurls
Columbus again and again,
sailing him out from Spain
to Indians and the New World.
His ships wear a track in the ocean.
Women and swords touch his name.
Europe swoons. For duty, devotion;
for bones, the eternal flame.
O memory, you tale-teller.
What do you need museums for
with all the burying-grounds around?

The vines weave coffins on the wall.
The War for Independence found
almost tears behind the pewter eyes,
swam like a fish into England,
was netted and overhauled to France.
The hawk at high noon whorls
through eddies of air like a sail in the sky,
then skiffs to harbor at dusk to die.
These books mirror my mind:
Boston Tea Party, Whisky Rebellion,
Daniel Shays, Civil War
war war war war.

I imagine I am a fish,
sticky, salted on Boston Common.
Later I will be Henry Adams,
play Sacco and Vanzetti,
tour Paris in a convertible Mercedes.
Now on a fog-filled night in the ice fields
off Cape Horn I hear
the groaning rigging in my sleep,
the bells tolling underneath
the windows of the fishes' tower.
The sea is a dark power.
I sing and I sing to the wind
as the world goes past its mind
beyond reason and fish and the sun's jellied eye.
Magnolia parachutes fall off the sky.
These boys, these vines, this white-petalled rain.
    Tonight I open a book
    as if opening my veins.

F. D. REEVE

NATIONAL SECURITY

There are three names
in a locked file
in a secret room
on a classified stair
in the house of state.

They are not to be spoken.

The first is old,
black and gold,
cool as lacquer
smelling of plums.
This name is Cambodia.

The second is Laos,
a flexible necklace
knotted with silver
sounds like the language
of orioles.

The third is Vietnam,
a dried child
mailed to its mother
by B-52s
in a cellophane envelope.

Three names
in a locked file
in a secret room
on a classified stair
in the house of state:
not to be spoken.

Nevertheless
the names bleed.
The blood runs out
under the secret
door and down
the classified stair
to the floor of state
and over the stoop
and out on the continent:
the country is steeped in it.

Not to be spoken.

ARCHIBALD MAC LEISH

"FAITH AND PRACTICE"

*Lo, I see four men loose, walking in the midst of the fire.—*DANIEL, *3:25**

Christians have always been pilgriming;
setting out with clamshell-hat and clapper;
begging barefoot and beating their backs;
hard seeking fellows, scabbing their skins;
swigging down wormwood, gulping down gall.
Just as soon would they fry on pyres
of martyrdom as bathe in a river of mercy.
Yet, ever since pitch-dipped Christians
lighted Nero's dinner parties, we have
understood the purgation of fire. Fire
shall come to roast up Babylon; fire shall
teach Ezekiel; fire shall light Job's pain.
Nowhere but in the bible of the spirit
could Shadrach, Meshach, and Abednego
crack jokes in Nebuchadnezzar's fiery furnace.
O Lord, I go into a land where napalm
makes men dance a crazy jig; where
Nero sets his sights by human flares.
I ask for clear water, good earth and air.

JOHN BALABAN

---

*A traditional Quaker text

143

THE FOUNDATIONS OF AMERICAN INDUSTRY

In the Ford plant
at Ypsilanti
men named for their
fathers work at steel
machines named Bliss,
Olaffson, Smith-Grieg,
and Safety.

In the Ford plant
the generators
move quickly on
belts, a thousand now
an hour. New men
move to the belt when
the shift comes.

For the most part
the men are young, and
go home to their
Fords, and drive around,
or watch TV,
sleep, and then go work,
towards payday;

when they walk home
they walk on sidewalks
marked W
P A 38;
their old men made
them, and they walk on
their fathers.

DONALD HALL

144

ON THE LAWN AT THE VILLA

On the lawn at the villa —
That's the way to start, eh, reader?
We know where we stand — somewhere expensive —
You and I *imperturbes*, as Walt would say,
Before the diversions of wealth, you and I *engagés*.

On the lawn at the villa
Sat a manufacturer of explosives,
His wife from Paris,
And a young man named Bruno,

And myself, being American,
Willing to talk to these malefactors,
The manufacturer of explosives, and so on,
But somehow superior. By that I mean democratic.
It's complicated, being an American,
Having the money and the bad conscience, both at the
    same time.
Perhaps, after all, this is not the right subject for a poem.

We were all sitting there paralyzed
In the hot Tuscan afternoon,
And the bodies of the machine-gun crew were draped
    over the balcony.
So we sat there all afternoon.

LOUIS SIMPSON

JUSTICE DENIED IN MASSACHUSETTS

Let us abandon then our gardens and go home
And sit in the sitting-room.
Shall the larkspur blossom or the corn grow under this cloud?
Sour to the fruitful seed
Is the cold earth under this cloud,
Fostering quack and weed, we have marched upon but cannot
    conquer;
We have bent the blades of our hoes against the stalks of them.

Let us go home, and sit in the sitting-room.
Not in our day
Shall the cloud go over and the sun rise as before,
Beneficent upon us
Out of the glittering bay,
And the warm winds be blown inward from the sea
Moving the blades of corn
With a peaceful sound.
Forlorn, forlorn,
Stands the blue hay-rack by the empty mow.
And the petals drop to the ground,
Leaving the tree unfruited.
The sun that warmed our stooping backs and withered the
    weed uprooted —
We shall not feel it again.
We shall die in darkness, and be buried in the rain.

Nicola Sacco and Bartolomeo Vanzetti, Italian immigrants, were executed
on August 22, 1927, for the murder of a paymaster and a guard of a shoe
factory. There was world-wide indignation and protests were sent to the
President and the Supreme Court because it seemed to the many thousand
protestors that Sacco and Vanzetti were executed because of their political
radicalism. They were anarchists.—H.P.

What from the splendid dead
We have inherited —
Furrows sweet to the grain, and the weed subdued —
See now the slug and the mildew plunder.
Evil does overwhelm
The larkspur and the corn;
We have seen them go under.

Let us sit here, sit still,
Here in the sitting-room until we die;
At the step of Death on the walk, rise and go;
Leaving to our children's children this beautiful doorway,
And this elm,
And a blighted earth to till
With a broken hoe.

EDNA ST. VINCENT MILLAY

from *TO ALEXANDER MEIKLEJOHN*

On the Occasion of His Senate Testimony in Defense of Liberty

I read your testimony and I thought
here is the man perfected that I knew
and reverenced next him who gave me life.
. . . .
. . . .
        The time is now for rising up
and speaking out our love. Know then, dear man,
that mine has grown beyond the hero worship
of youth when your ideas broke the mould
of prejudice in which my mind was formed.
You let the world in on me, were the yeast
that set me boiling with desire to know
not merely but to do. I thought I loved
my country. You taught why America
deserved my love and all mankind's because
America was more than just a land;
it was the sum of all that men had won
against the ancient darkness. So believing
my life grew meaningful and where before
I felt myself an atom in the void
I now engaged to join with other men
to keep the light alive and specially
to oppose all those who in the name of light
would re-enthrone the darkness and betray
America. This they have nearly done.

Alexander Meiklejohn was a great American educator. In testimony before
the Henning Subcommittee on Constitutional Liberty in 1946, he said: "To be
afraid of any idea is to be unfit for self-government. Any such suppression
of ideas about the common good, the First Amendment condemns with its
absolute disapproval. The freedom of ideas shall not be abridged." He was
awarded the Medal of Freedom in 1963.—H.P.

And I myself in prime of life have felt
the anguished bitterness that exiles know
cut off and cast away. How easy now
to curse America, cast in one's lot
with enemies, back one usurping gang
against the other! But for you I think
I would have made this all-too-human error.
Despised, rejected as I felt, the thought
of you restrained me at the brink. "What would
he think? What would he do himself?" So clear
the answer always came. "Believe!" you said,
"Don't let them drive you to despair! Fight on!"

JOHN BEECHER

SPEECH FOR THE REPEAL
OF THE McCARRAN ACT

As Wulfstan said on another occasion,
The strong net bellies in the wind and the spider rides it out;
But history, that sure blunderer,
Ruins the unkempt web, however silver.

I am not speaking of rose windows
Shattered by bomb-shock; the leads touselled; the glass-grains
 broadcast;
If the rose be living at all
A gay gravel shall be pollen of churches.

Nor do I mean railway networks.
Torn-up tracks are no great trouble. As Wulfstan said,
It is oathbreach, faithbreach, lovebreach
Bring the invaders into the estuaries.

Shall one man drive before him ten
Unstrung from sea to sea? Let thought be free. I speak
Of the spirit's weaving, the neural
Web, the self-true mind, the trusty reflex.

RICHARD WILBUR

The McCarran Immigration Act, passed June 27, 1952, retained the national-origins quota for immigrants, allowing more than two-thirds of the total to the United Kingdom, Germany and Ireland. It also provided rigorous screening of aliens in order to exclude subversives and broadened the grounds for deportation of "criminal aliens." The bill was vetoed by President Truman.
—H.P.

BELIEF

for JFK

1

drums gather and humble us beyond escape,
propound the single, falling fact:
time, suspended between memory and present,
hangs unmeasured, empty

2

erect,
disciplined by cadence into direction, the soldier
obeys the forms of rumor:
the riderless horse,
restive with the pressure of held flight,
tosses the hung bit,
worries the soldier's tameless arm —
sidling, prances the energy out

3

ahead, unalterable, the fact proceeds,
and the bit holds:
the fire-needle bites,
training the head on course

4

the light, determined rattle
of the caisson
breaking into sunlight
through the crystal black ribbons of trees!
the slack traces,
weightlessness at the shoulders of horses!

5

if we could break free
and run this knowledge out
burst this energy of grief
through a hundred countrysides!
if bleak through the black night
we could outrun
this knowledge into a different morning!

6

belief, light as a drumrattle,
touches us and lifts us up to tears.

A. R. AMMONS

MONTICELLO

This legendary house, this dear enchanted tomb,
Once so supremely lived in, and for life designed,
Will none of moldy death nor give it room,
Charged with the presence of a living mind.

Enter, and touch the temper of a lively man.
See, it is spacious, intimate and full of light.
The eye, pleased by detail, is nourished by the plan;
Nothing is here for show, much for delight.

All the joys of invention and of craft and wit,
Are freely granted here, all given rein,
But taut within the classic form and ruled by it,
Elegant, various, magnificent — and plain,

Europe become implacably American!
Yet Mozart could have been as happy here,
As Monroe riding from his farm again,
As well as any silversmith or carpenter —

As well as we, for whom this elegance,
This freedom in a form, this peaceful grace,
Is not our heritage, although it happened once:
We read the future, not the past, upon his face.

MAY SARTON

Yes, yes, yes, yes

※ *IDEA OF*
AMERICA

AMERICA THE BEAUTIFUL

O beautiful for spacious skies,
  For amber waves of grain,
For purple mountain majesties
  Above the fruited plain!
America! America!
  God shed His grace on thee
And crown thy good with brotherhood
  From sea to shining sea!

O beautiful for pilgrim feet,
  Whose stern, impassioned stress
A thoroughfare for freedom beat
  Across the wilderness!
America! America!
  God mend thine every flaw,
Confirm thy soul in self-control,
  Thy liberty in law!

O beautiful for heroes proved
  In liberating strife,
Who more than self their country loved,
  And mercy more than life!
America! America!
  May God thy gold refine,
Till all success be nobleness
  And every gain divine!

O beautiful for patriot dream
    That sees beyond the years
Thine alabaster cities gleam
    Undimmed by human tears!
America! America!
    God shed His grace on thee,
And crown thy good with brotherhood
    From sea to shining sea!

KATHARINE LEE BATES

LYRIC

From now on kill America out of your mind.
America is dead these hundred years.
You've better work to do, and things to find.
   Waste neither time nor tears.

See rather, all the millions and all the land
Mutually shapen as a child of love.
As individual as a hand.
   And to be thought highly of.

The wrinkling mountains stay: the master stream
Still soils the Gulf a hundred amber miles:
A people as a creature in a dream
   Not yet awakened, smiles.

Those poisons which were low along the air
like mists, like mists are lifting. Even now
Thousands are breathing health in, here and there:
   Millions are learning how.

JAMES AGEE

BENJAMIN FRANKLIN HAZARD

You built the new Court House, Spoon River,
You laid one stone upon another —
But what made them stay? Was it the mortar only?
You put in arches, and groined ceilings —
What held them up? Was it the material,
Or the placing of material obedient to laws?
Who made those laws, who compelled you,
Even if you wanted neither air nor light,
Not to make vacuums of rooms, lest they collapse?
What do I mean, I who preached Americanism?
I am hitting at Americanism, laws, constitutions.
Can you make laws and constitutions the way you want to,
Against soul gravitations, arches without keys?
Rooms without air?
Or must you make them according to the laws of the soul?
What is The Law, the constitution, or the law of the soul?
What is Americanism? I tell you:
It is to be an Athenian, an Atlantian:
Free, joyous, harmonious, balanced,
Simple, just, tolerant, wise,
Peaceful, loving beauty,
Unprejudiced, seeking to learn,
Devoted to nature, and to the happiness that comes from these,
And a maker of new gods in the image of perfected hope,
And adoration!

EDGAR LEE MASTERS

MEREDITH PHYFE

Come now! You supercilious detractors of America
As a land of aridity, without stories and myths,
Without romance, without epic material:
Did not Brigham Young found as good a religion as
    Henry VIII,
And build a greater city than Henry VIII ever built?
Are not the Forty-niners, the Oregon Trailers,
The Daniel Boones and the Sam Houstons
As full of pictures as the Crusaders?
Did not the Fathers, so called,
Accomplish as much as the knights of the Table Round?
Are not Carrie Nation and Mary Ellen Leese
As mad and significant as Joan of Arc?
Was any war of Europe
Bloodier or more momentous than the Revolution,
Or the Civil War?
And why dream about Peter the Hermit
With John Brown under your nose?
Is Robin Hood a fitter subject for ballads
Than Jesse James?
And have we not had Dowies and Schlatterys and Bryans
By the score,
With every variety of religionists
From Shakers to Holy Rollers?
What do you want for irony, satire or pathos?
Is there not every thing here, grotesque,
Absurd, tragic and heroic?

Have you not seen in your own life
More than twenty states acquire more than two million people,
And several cities acquire more than that number of souls,
and dozens of cities acquire a half million or more?
Have you not seen mountains climbed, railroads built,
Iron and coal mastered,
Over this vast stretch of restless, crazy humanity?
Is the Woolworth building nothing,
And St. Peter's everything?
Think it over,
You supercilious dreamers of dead days!

EDGAR LEE MASTERS

ADDRESS TO THE SCHOLARS
OF NEW ENGLAND

(Harvard Phi Beta Kappa Poem, June 23, 1939)

When Sarah Pierrepont let her spirit rage
Her love and scorn refused the bauble earth
(Which took bloom even here, under the Bear)
And groped for the Essence sitting in himself,
Subtle, I think, for a girl's unseasoned rage.

The late and sudden extravagance of soul
By which they all were swollen exalted her
At seventeen years to Edwards' canopy,
A match pleasing to any Heaven, had not
The twelve mortal labors harassed her soul.

Thrifty and too proud were the sea-borne fathers
Who fetched the Pure Idea in a bound box
And fastened him in a steeple, to have his court
Shabby with an unkingly establishment
And Sabbath levees for the minion fathers.

The majesty of Heaven has a great house,
And even if the Indian kingdom or the fox
Ran barking mad in a wide forest place,
They had his threshold, and you had the dream
Of property in him by a steepled house.

Sarah Pierrepont married the Puritan theologian Jonathan Edwards in 1727.
He said of her, "She has a strange sweetness in her mind, and singular purity
in her affections; is most just and conscientious in all her conduct; . . . She
will sometimes go about from place to place, singing sweetly, and seems to
be always full of joy and pleasure, and no one knows for what. She loves to
be alone, walking in the fields and groves, and seems to have some one invis-
ible always conversing with her."—H.P.

If once the entail shall come on raffish sons,
Knife-wit scholar and merchant sharp in thumb,
With positive steel they'll pry into the steeple,
And blinking through the cracked ribs at the void
A judgment laughter rakes the cynic sons.

But like prevailing wind New England's honor
Carried, and teased small Southern boys in school,
Whose heads the temperate birds fleeing your winter
Construed for, but the stiff heroes abashed
With their frozen fingers and unearthly honor.

Scared by the holy megrims of those Pilgrims,
I thought the unhumbled and outcast and cold
Were the rich Heirs traveling incognito,
Bred too fine for the country's sweet produce
And but affecting that dog's life of pilgrims.

There used to be debate of soul and body,
The soul storming incontinent with shrew's tongue
Against what natural brilliance body had loved,
Even the green phases though deciduous
Of earth's zodiac homage to the body.

Plato, before Plotinus gentled him,
Spoke the soul's part, and though its vice is known
We're in his shadow still, and it appears
Your founders most of all the nations held
By his scandal-mongering, and established him.

Perfect was the witch foundering in water,
The blasphemer that spraddled in the stocks,
The woman branded with her sin, the whales
Of ocean taken with a psalmer's sword,
The British tea infusing the bay's water.

But they reared heads into the always clouds
And stooped to the event of war or bread,
The secular perforces and short speech
Being labors surlily done with the left hand,
The chief strength giddying with transcendent clouds.

The tangent Heavens mocked the fathers' strength,
And how the young sons know it, and study now
To take fresh conquest of the conquered earth,
But they're too strong for that, you've seen them whip
The laggard will to deeds of lunatic strength.

To incline the powerful living unto peace
With Heaven is easier now, with Earth is hard,
Yet a rare metaphysic makes them one,
A gentle Majesty, whose myrtle and rain
Enforce the fathers' gravestones unto peace.

I saw the youngling bachelors of Harvard
Lit like torches, and scrambling to disperse
Like aimless firebrands pitiful to slake,
And if there's passion enough for half their flame,
Your wisdom has done this, sages of Harvard.

JOHN CROWE RANSOM

PATRUM PROPOSITUM*
for W. M.

Bewildered in our buying throng,
    What came of it too well we know,
Of Santa Fe and Oregon,
    Of Adams, Jefferson, Monroe.

The Fathers' influences abate;
    And yet they live in the mind's eye,
Their ancient quest and craft of state
    Essences above history,

Elated, practical, and proud —
    As in high air to a small boy,
In August, wagon trains of cloud
    Bear westward over Illinois.

ROBERT FITZGERALD

---

*Design of the fathers—H.P.

LONG, TOO LONG AMERICA

Long, too long America,
Traveling roads all even and peaceful you learn'd from joys
    and prosperity only,
But now, ah now, to learn from crises of anguish, advancing,
    grappling with direst fate and recoiling not,
And now to conceive and show to the world what your
    children en-masse really are,
(For who except myself has yet conceiv'd what your children
    en-masse really are?)

WALT WHITMAN

ODE

God save the Rights of Man!
Give us a heart to scan
Blessings so dear:
Let them be spread around
Wherever man is found,
And with the welcome sound
Ravish his ear.

Let us with France agree,
And bid the world be free,
While tyrants fall!
Let the rude savage host
Of their vast numbers boast —
Freedom's almighty trust
Laughs at them all!

Though hosts of slaves conspire
To quench fair Gallia's fire,
Still shall they fail:
Though traitors round her rise,
Leagu'd with her enemies,
To war each patriot flies,
And will prevail.

No more is valor's flame
Devoted to a name,
Taught to adore —
Soldiers of Liberty
Disdain to bow the knee,
But teach Equality
To every shore.

The world at last will join
To aid thy grand design,
Dear Liberty!
To Russia's frozen lands
The generous flame expands:
On Afric's burning sands
Shall man be free!

In this our western world
Be Freedom's flag unfurl'd
Through all its shores!
May no destructive blast
Our heaven of joy o'ercast,
May Freedom's fabric last
While time endures.

If e'er her cause require! —
Should tyrants e'er aspire
To aim their stroke,
May no proud despot daunt —
Should he his standard plant,
Freedom will never want
Her hearts of oak!

PHILIP FRENEAU

AMERICA

Centre of equal daughters, equal sons,
All, all alike endear'd, grown, ungrown, young or old,
Strong, ample, fair, enduring, capable, rich,
Perennial with the Earth, with Freedom, Law and Love,
A grand, sane, towering, seated Mother,
Chair'd in the adamant of Time.

WALT WHITMAN

SHINE, REPUBLIC

The quality of these trees, green height; of the sky, shining,
   of water, a clear flow; of the rock, hardness
And reticence: each is noble in its quality. The love of
   freedom has been the quality of Western man.

There is a stubborn torch that flames from Marathon to
   Concord, its dangerous beauty binding three ages
Into one time; the waves of barbarism and civilization have
   eclipsed but have never quenched it.

For the Greeks the love of beauty, for Rome of ruling;
   for the present age the passionate love of discovery;
But in one noble passion we are one; and Washington,
   Luther, Tacitus, Aeschylus, one kind of man.

And you, America, that passion made you. You were not born
   to prosperity, you were born to love freedom.
You did not say "en masse," you said "independence."
   But we cannot have all the luxuries and freedom also.

Freedom is poor and laborious; that torch is not safe but
   hungry, and often requires blood for its fuel.
You will tame it against it burn too clearly, you will hood it
   like a kept hawk, you will perch it on the wrist of Caesar.

But keep the tradition, conserve the forms, the observances,
   keep the spot sore. Be great, carve deep your heel-marks.
The states of the next age will no doubt remember you,
   and edge their love of freedom with contempt of luxury.

ROBINSON JEFFERS

from *A NEW YEAR LETTER*

A long time since it seems to-day
The Saints in Massachusetts Bay
Heard theocratic *Cotton* preach
And legal *Winthrop's* Little Speech.
Since *Mistress Hutchinson* was tried
By those her Inner Light defied
And *Williams* questioned Moses' law
But in Rhode Island waited for
The Voice of the Beloved to free
Himself and the Democracy,
Long since inventive *Jefferson*
Fought realistic *Hamilton*,
Pelagian versus Jansenist;
But the same heresies exist:
Time makes old formulas look strange,
Our properties and symbols change,
But round the freedom of the Will
Our disagreements centre still,
And now as then the voter hears
The battle cries of two ideas.
Here, as in Europe, is dissent,
This raw untidy continent
Where the Commuter can't forget
The Pioneer; and even yet
A Völkerwanderung occurs:

Resourceful manufacturers
Trek southward by progressive stages
For sites with no floor under wages,
No ceiling over hours; and by
Artistic souls in towns that lie
Out in the weed and pollen belt
The need for sympathy is felt
And east to hard New York they come;
And self-respect drives negroes from
The one-crop and race-hating delta
To northern cities helter-skelter:
And in jalopies there migrates
A rootless tribe from windblown states
To suffer further westward, where
The tolerant Pacific air
Makes logic seem so silly, pain
Subjective, what he seeks so vain
The wanderer may die; and kids
When their imagination bids
Hitch-hike a thousand miles to find
The Hesperides that's on their mind,
Some Texas where real cowboys seem
Lost in a movie-cowboy's dream.
More even than in Europe, here
The choice of patterns is made clear
Which the machine imposes, what
Is possible and what is not,
To what conditions we must bow
In building the Just City now.

W. H. AUDEN

I AM WAITING

I am waiting for my case to come up
and I am waiting
for a rebirth of wonder
and I am waiting for someone
to really discover America
and wail
and I am waiting
for the discovery
of a new symbolic western frontier
and I am waiting
for the American Eagle
to really spread its wings
and straighten up and fly right
and I am waiting
for the Age of Anxiety
to drop dead
and I am waiting
for the war to be fought
which will make the world safe
for anarchy
and I am waiting
for the final withering away
of all governments
and I am perpetually awaiting
a rebirth of wonder

LAWRENCE FERLINGHETTI

[This is one of] seven poems [that] were conceived specifically for jazz
accompaniment and as such should be considered as spontaneously spoken
"oral messages" rather than as poems written for the printed page. As a re-
sult of continued experimental reading with jazz, they are still in a state of
change.—L.F.

FARE THEE WELL

Oh, mighty America, hast thou come to this?
Has all thy grandeur, all thy hopes, all thy wonder,
Thy Bradford and thy Franklin,
Thy Whitman and thy Boone,
Thy Cooper and thy Norris,
Thy London and thy Debs,
Thy Jane Addams and thy sunrise —
Come to this?
That thou shouldst be looked on with terror
By an unknown child in Asia? —
Fare thee well, O land, fare thee other.

ELI SIEGEL

THE BUILDING
OF THE SKYSCRAPER

The steel worker on the girder
Learned not to look down, and does his work
And there are words we have learned
Not to look at,
Not to look for substance
Below them. But we are on the verge
Of vertigo.

There are words that mean nothing
But there is something to mean.
Not a declaration which is truth
But a thing
Which is. It is the business of the poet
'To suffer the things of the world
And to speak them and himself out.'

O, the tree, growing from the sidewalk—
It has a little life, sprouting
Little green buds
Into the culture of the streets.
We look back
Three hundred years and see bare land.
And suffer vertigo.

GEORGE OPPEN

LIBERTY

When liberty is headlong girl
And runs her roads and wends her ways
Liberty will shriek and whirl
Her showery torch to see it blaze.

When liberty is wedded wife
And keeps the barn and counts the byre
Liberty amends her life.
She drowns her torch for fear of fire.

ARCHIBALD MAC LEISH

YONDER

I held Europe in my hand
Like a jewel that is implacable.
When I became most interior
I fled to my native land;

I returned to America, singing
Poets dead, long-living causes;
I loved them all. About them
I felt hypocoristical.

When the lovers walk on the Danube
And the thinkers vie in the park
I give my hand to the Big Horns,
I seek the Pacific in the dark.

RICHARD EBERHART

MINORITY REPORT

My beloved land,
here I sit in London
   overlooking Regent's Park
   overlooking my new Citroën } both green,
exiled by success of sorts.
I listen to Mozart
  in my English suit and weep,
    remembering a Swedish film.
But it is you,
  really you I think of:
    your nothing streetcorners
    your ugly eateries
    your dear barbarities
    and vacant lots
(Br'er Rabbit demonstrated:
    freedom is made of brambles).
They say over here you are choking
  to death on your cities and slaves,
    but they have never smelled dry grass,
    smoked Kools in a drugstore,
    or pronounced a flat "a," an honest "r."
Don't read your reviews,
A ☆ M ☆ E ☆ R ☆ I ☆ C ☆ A:
you are the only land.

JOHN UPDIKE

LOVE IN AMERICA?

Whatever it is, it's a passion—
a benign dementia that should be
engulfing America, fed in a way
   the opposite of the way
in which the Minotaur was fed.
It's a Midas of tenderness;
   from the heart;
nothing else. From one with ability
to bear being misunderstood—
   take the blame, with "nobility
   that is action," identifying itself with
   pioneer unperfunctoriness

   without brazenness or
   bigness of overgrown
   undergrown shallowness.

Whatever it is, let it be without
   affectation.

Yes, yes, yes, *yes*.

MARIANNE MOORE

180

※※ *INDEXES*

INDEX TO AUTHORS

C

Clifton, Lucille (1936–   ), 44
Coatsworth, Elizabeth (1893–   ), 8
Crane, Hart (1899–1932), 88

D

Dickey, James (1923–   ), 136
Dickinson, Emily (1830–1886), 118
Dorman, Sonya, 62, 68

E

Eberhart, Richard (1904–   ), 15, 178
Emerson, Ralph Waldo (1803–1882), 117, 125

F

Ferlinghetti, Lawrence (1920–   ), 174
Fitzgerald, Robert (1910–   ), 166
Francis, Robert (1901–   ), 20
Freneau, Philip (1752–1832), 25, 50, 111, 168
Frost, Robert (1874–1963), xvii, 37

G

Gregory, Horace (1898–   ), 9

H

Hall, Donald (1928–   ), 144
Hayden, Robert E. (1913–   ), 122
Heyen, William (1940–   ), 99
Holmes, Oliver Wendell (1809–1891), 119
Hughes, Langston (1902–1967), 53

J

Jarrell, Randall (1914–1965), 39
Jeffers, Robinson (1887–1962), 23, 31, 171
Johnson, Edward (1598–1672), 41

INDEX TO TITLES

INDEX TO FIRST LINES

D

E

F

G

H

I

ACKNOWLEDGMENTS

Thanks are due to the following for permission to include copyrighted poems:

Atheneum Publishers, Inc. for "Jamestown" from *The Woman at the Washington Zoo* by Randall Jarrell, Copyright © 1960 by Randall Jarrell; "The Trail into Kansas" from *The Carrier of Ladders* by W. S. Merwin, Copyright © 1967, 1968, 1969, 1970 by W. S. Merwin; and "You, Genoese Mariner" from *The First Four Books of Poems* by W. S. Merwin, Copyright © 1954, 1975 by W. S. Merwin (this poem originally appeared in *Dancing Bears* by W. S. Merwin).

Carlos Baker for "The Men of Sudbury" from *A Year and a Day* by Carlos Baker, Copyright © 1963 by Carlos Baker.

Ben Belitt, for "The Sand Painters" from *The Enemy Joy: New and Selected Poems* by Ben Belitt, Copyright © 1964 by The University of Chicago Press.

Brandt & Brandt for "Daniel Boone" and "American Names" by Stephen Vincent Benét from *A Book of Americans* by Rosemary and Stephen Vincent Benét (Holt, Rinehart and Winston, Inc.), Copyright, 1933, by Rosemary and Stephen Vincent Benét, Copyright renewed, 1961, by Rosemary Carr Benét.

John Malcolm Brinnin for "A New England Sampler" and "Address to the Refugees" from *The Garden Is Political*, Copyright 1942; and "American Plan" from *The Sorrows of Cold Stone*, Copyright 1951.

Edited by Helen Plotz

THOMAS Y. CROWELL CO.

The Earth Is the Lord's:
Poems of the Spirit

Imagination's Other Place:
Poems of Science and Mathematics

Poems from the German

Poems of Emily Dickinson

Poems of Robert Louis Stevenson

Untune the Sky:
Poems of Music and the Dance

The Marvelous Light:
Poets and Poetry

MACMILLAN PUBLISHING CO., INC.

The Pinnacled Tower:
Selected Poems of Thomas Hardy

GREENWILLOW BOOKS

As I Walked Out One Evening:
A Book of Ballads

The Gift Outright:
America to Her Poets